The Cost of Our Baggage
Copyright 2024 Gnashing Teeth Publishing

Original Cover Art by

The font used is Times New Roman
The cover font is

Gnashing Teeth Publishing
242 East Main Street
Norman AR 71960
rights@gnashingteethpublishing.com

Printed in the United States of America

ISBN 979-8-9898345-8-7

Fiction: Anthology

Gnashing Teeth Publishing First Edition

The Cost of Our Baggage

the haunting of grief
Katie Hébert

A lullaby echoes in dusty hallways
Your sharp commands transforming into a raspy groan

The speech therapist tried to help you pronounce the pain
But the radiation swallowed your windpipe;

      Already fading.

Haunted your brain before you could invite it in

I smell the ashes of it in the musk of the transverse
The days blurring together like the memory of your voice

I know you loved the beach
Is the saltwater washing away your face?

Do you know what you crawl for any more or is it just routine,
this wanting and aching for something that will never return?

I hear your footsteps slowly making their way to the next room
A lightbulb flickers but there is no   body.

Just a box of ashes on the mantle, just a framed portrait
waiting to break through the house, just a lineage

Erasing itself.

For the first few weeks after, I felt a hand rub my back as I slept
In an empty room.
Are you reaching for me?
Are you walking around to find me?

Mom, do you yearn for the daughter
your body got separated from?

Cape House
Laurel Galford

Her family has invited you to their Cape house.

Well, technically it's in Wareham, which if you ask anyone who lives past the Bourne bridge, will tell you this is *not* Cape Cod. This technicality doesn't matter, because it's the *good* side of Wareham, and your family just visits the cape. *You are tourists,* she says. *You don't count.*

She can't wait to show you the house and you can't wait to see this part of her life, a piece she wants to share with you, a piece she also shared with the girls before you. You don't care, you are just happy to be here. It's small but the *perfect beach shack*, it gets the *crosswinds just right so there's always a breeze,* she says to you over, and over again. But now more people are moving closer, blocking their view of the water. She sighs, *people just ruin everything.*

It is fun at first, being with her family, there is always an inside joke, quick banter you try to keep up with. It's nice how open they are around you, so open that they don't mind gossiping about close friends or family, people they care about. They reveal secrets and hypocrisies and report that the neighbors want to be just like them. *Really, isn't it so strange? How jealous people are?* You nod along, your head empty of any response, happy to be here.

The family gives you beer and wine, one of each to keep up with both the father and the mother, who has a heavy pour, but you don't mind. They drink so you drink. One day you drink too much and can't stop sharing about your own family, even when you see their eyes glazing over. The next morning you are nursing a hangover when she tells you how *embarrassing* that was for her.

You sit on the couch that has begun to sink from where the dog sprawls on top of the cushions. You all coo at the dog like a baby, he is a sweet boy, but he is not your dog, so he's a little less cute to you because of it. You try to bring up your own dog at home, the one whose tail is probably thumping in the rhythm of her missing you. But she is not their dog, so she is less cute because of it. You focus on their dog and agree, he's the cutest dog you've ever met.

You are three months into your relationship which so far consists of drinking, fucking, board games, reruns of *The Office*, fucking and walking her dog. You exist in both the beginning of knowing each other and a routine that was easy to slip into, like a coma. You laugh at the insensitive jokes she makes, even the ones at your expense. Your last relationship lost all laughter in the end, you want to be carefree now, happy. She knows you're a feminist, raised with liberal values and spiritual parents, but her brand is offensive humor. You decide you can be the chill girlfriend until you are strong enough to correct her (later when you do, she will roll her eyes and accuse you of being *too sensitive*).

She is cool, her clothes are preppy casual and never wrinkled. She is spontaneous and personable; you eat at all her favorite restaurants, meet her family and friends, who report that they like you. She shows you things you never cared to try before, like rock climbing (one time she laughs and leaves you hanging high up, your voice cracks as you beg to come back down), IPAs (you've always thought they tasted like dirt), and tribbing (it's her favorite position, she loves to get off).

Sometimes she is confusing, asks you to drive but criticizes you so much that you give up and let her take the wheel (then she will complain how she is *always* driving). Shows you off to her friends then complains about them on the way home. Tells you you're beautiful, but after dinner says you both should do hot yoga *to sweat the weight off*. You try to stay happy.

Back at the cape house, the shower is a source of pride for her dad--*the water pressure is amazing*. She makes sure you remember to mention it. The shower is volcanic, the pressure beats against your skin, the steam makes you sweat more. The shower is tiny, you knock your elbows into the walls when you wash your hair. The shower is the only moment of solitude you get, except for that one time she barged in, drunk, laughing as she took up the remaining space.

The shower is in the bathroom, which is right next to the kitchen, which is attached to the living area which is most of the small home. You are often constipated when visiting because of how much you dread shitting in proximity to everyone. But *yes* you agree, *the water pressure is amazing*. You are so lucky to be here.

You are not like her first ex-girlfriend, the one she talks about in what-ifs, *what if* the ex had never moved down south, *what if* they had moved in together. The ex who loved to cook with her (and knew how to do it well, unlike you), the ex who had a *great ass but a butter face* which you had never heard of before because it's a misogynistic term only boys use. You don't hang out with misogynists. This will not be the first time you realize she is One of the Boys, as in loves women in a sexist way and thinks being the devil's advocate is fun. One of the Boys, as in a lesbian who laughs at jokes where gay people are the punchline, who uses her physical strength to both protect and intimidate you. She feels like the closest thing you will get to dating a man, the closest thing you get to being a little afraid of your partner.

You are reminded of the frog who doesn't notice the temperature of the water is rising. You are so happy, boiling to death.

And you aren't like her second ex-girlfriend, the one she cheated on her first girlfriend with, the same one she cheated on later, *well we cheated on each other*. That ex had a broken childhood, drank too much, the sex was angry and chaotic, *amazing*. Sometimes they hit each other. You don't hit each other, but once in a while you fall asleep dreaming about smashing the windows of her car. It surprises you the way you let her speak to you later in the relationship. How your family doesn't have a Cape house but *could* have, your education isn't impressive, your job, a joke. She says she blacked out during most of college, dreams of being a landlord, likes the idea of ownership, of control.

She is not like your ex-girlfriend, the one who helped you love yourself, the one you don't admit you still miss. And she is not like the other ex-girlfriend, the one who was quiet in a way you admired first and later came to resent. You felt like you couldn't get her to talk, to open up. In this relationship there is so much openness it is like a wound. She is not afraid to tell you what is wrong with you, not afraid to remind you to be grateful of all that she does for you. There is less air in the room for you to talk back so instead, you listen.

The family gives you a shirt with the name of their boat on it. You are honored, make sure they know how special you feel, how part of the family you feel. Once for Mother's Day you leave early in the morning and they are disappointed you won't stay, but you have your own mom to see, your own family to love. They frown as you leave. Sometimes you feel like every weekend is with this family, this family who is not really your family. She rarely comes to stay with you. Then again, your family doesn't have a boat or a Cape house.

You smile, the shirt is tight on you, they want to include you in things. They act as if it's a crime that you've never been on a sailboat, but you've *been on ferries and kayaks* you tell them, *it's not the same, this is more fun.* But you have to be careful about what shoes you wear, careful not to scratch or dirty it, feel like you can't relax until they tell you when to. She jokes her dad *loves the boat more than his kids.*

They tell you about boat safety and you listen. They tell you a story of a girl they know whose arm got cut off from the propellers, so *safety is a priority, she wasn't with good people.* When you are sitting in the attached beach floats, the father moves the boat, turning on the propellers near you, and you jump out immediately. Your drink spills into the ocean, you drown briefly and come up with lungs full of water. They laugh, they must have forgotten the story they just told you. The one about good people.

They tell you the best way to enjoy the ocean, to enjoy food, which happens to be their family way. You stop offering your own opinions when you realize no one is listening. She reminds you to be grateful of all her family does for you. You didn't ask for this. Your life does not suffer from not having a boat or a Cape house, but she doesn't seem to believe you (and when you become defensive she will tell you, *you have mommy issues*).

Back at the house everyone is comfortably buzzed, well she is hammered, without you noticing she had ten White Claws to herself and everyone is laughing. You aren't as relaxed, this is not your home or your family, not your dog or your shower. They pick the movie to watch and later she will pick the position she fucks you in. You are so easy-going you stop making a sound. You can't remember why you try so hard to fit in here.

They convince you to try an oyster with mustard and hot sauce. You tell them you don't like oysters or hot sauce, but she says it's her dad's favorite and don't you want to impress? Grateful to be shown these pieces of her, (pieces you're not even sure you like)? You let the father feed you the oyster and grimace as the slime slips down your throat. You wash it down quickly with the beer you hate and, politely say *thank you but it's not for me*. They laugh at your expression, at your bravery, your ability to stomach something you don't want. *I was just messing with you,* she says, *my dad hates them too.*

December 29, 2021 Near Central Houston
Edward Garza

Slipping Away
Andrea Yarbough

Time has turned away from me.

I am reminded of this daily as I walk past my son's room, catch sight of the plastic bag sitting on a dusty corner of his dresser. Inside the bag lies his future—and my regrets. I always thought regrets would be larger: the lover you didn't marry, the job you didn't wait for. I know better now. But it's too late. The plastic bag sitting on the dusty corner of my son's dresser tells me that regrets are not an unwillingness to take risks, but a failure to take time, time that is not measured by the ticking of the clock or the waning of the moon, but in the moments of inaction when opportunity slips away over a glass of orange juice at breakfast. Moments when the sun rises over a bare patch of dirt nestled among the trees.

A treehouse used to rise above that ground, hovering broken over our heads like a dream you can't quite piece together. I don't know how long it had been there. Long enough to fall apart, I guess. Our children never played in it. We had dreams of rebuilding it— shoring it up so they could climb to the sky while they were still young enough to soar. But the house on the ground needed work and so we turned to that instead, promising our children that we would fix the treehouse soon.

A few years ago, we tore the treehouse down. It was too old, and now our kids were, too. The season of treehouses had passed. Now it was time for woodland obstacle courses and forested battles.

My son's room overlooks that patch of dirt in the trees. I found him one day, sketching his dreams, a massive wooden structure for him to climb, jump, and scale. He showed it to us. Wouldn't it be amazing? He told us he was learning woodworking in school and could help dad build it. They could go outside and train together when it was finished. My son dreams big. But our bank account was small. His dreams would have to wait until we could afford all that wood.

He threw the sketch away a while back after coming across it in his closet. "Remember this, mom," he asked with a chuckle. Yes. That was only yesterday, I thought to myself as I watched him trash the page.

The plastic bag arrived a few days ago. It holds his cap and gown. My son will be graduating in a few short weeks and I realize now that my yesterday is his distant childhood and I wish someone had told me how differently time moves for children than it does for adults. I wish I had known that every glass of orange juice was a year of his life and I was drinking it away with the idea that tomorrow there would be time. But now tomorrow has come and gone and soon he will be walking across the stage and the patch of dirt nestled among the trees is still bare because I was too busy to build the dreams I had promised him. Now he must build his own.

I sip my juice and think that tomorrow I will tell him how sorry I am.

Self Portrait At Age Five
Heidi Spitzig

Every day but Saturday is spent at church
or school, which is the same place, which is to say praying
was a skill I was failing since my prayers were never answered.

In my dreams, men in dark suits wear crosses.
They eat the body of Christ, drink his blood. In daylight,
I hide from them in gym lockers, closets, lock myself in bathrooms.

I'm not quite a self yet. I wear my father's sadness as my own.
I am my mother's obsession and compulsion, a forever filthy
thing she can't scrub clean to relieve her suffering.

Our house is pristine because I spend every Saturday
on my knees, my small hands dusting, scrubbing, polishing,
my fate as fragile as a glass slipper that never arrives.

My brother's body shrinks as he runs down the road.
I try to escape after him. I'm halfway out the window when my father grabs
my ankles to pull me back into his screaming red face devil embrace.

I make a home inside myself to escape
the one I can't leave. It's haunted by voices.
I give each one a name.

Breasts, at Summer Camp, at 11, Listening to Come on Eileen
Billie Sainwood

During lunch the counselors played classic rock
while we ate and hummed along,
until the day "Come on Eileen" came on

and one of the campers or counselors
(I don't remember)
stood up on the dining bench,
whipped his shirt off,
and twirled it over his head.

It was funny, and weird,
and then we all stood,
even me with my second helping of dessert,
even me with my awkward about swimming class,
and never running in case somebody saw me,
and laughed,

We all burst from our shirts, sweaty and foolish
cheap cotton helicopters dancing crazy
for as long as the song let us.
No one was too big for shirtless,
too fat for fun,
too embarrassed to twirl
or look like a girl.

Everyone was a blown dandelion
scattered in summer air.

And then it was over
and our shirts limped back onto our bodies
and I was boy and bare skin again
naked under my clothes
all shiver and shame.

Within minutes
another song was playing
something about being a man
and strong and muscular guitars,
like nothing had happened.

Binge
Kathleen Latham

That was the year my friend Lisa tried to eat
all her Halloween candy in one night
because her mother said

Whatever's left over is going in the trash.
She said, Five pounds this month, ten pounds next.
She said, Might as well glue that candy to your ass.

We were eleven years old with no breasts
to speak of, no hips, no waists, no sense
of proportion, trying too hard in our hippie

costumes, nail polish peace signs drawn
on our jeans, colored beads *tsking*
against our flat chests as we scurried to hide

Reese's peanut butter cups under Lisa's mattress,
Crunch bars in her shoes, packets of M&M's
in her underwear drawer.

We stopped going door to door the next year,
kept up the rest—the masks, the tricks,
the ritual pretending.

Fun size bites of judgment stashed away,
waiting to remind us of wanting.
Of secrets. Of shame.

Brother
Erin Jamieson

You were always going to leave my life- it was a question of when.

Summer days running barefoot through sprinklers, sharing sliced PB&J sandwiches and Wheat Thins at our pool; the beauty of sculpting misaligned snow forts out of the first snowfall.

When Mom was pregnant, you asked for a sister. You wanted to name me Sister Willy, but when Mom told you they were *all out of that name,* you said Erin was fine.

You were gentle, eager to share- except for Easter Egg Hunts. I often found the pastel eggs first, only for you to nudge me out of the way.

I suppose it makes sense now. How, despite the years of memories we shared, despite you being there for me when I was hospitalized, there came a time where I no longer fit.

Permission Slips
Shelly Reed Thieman

For thirteen years of life, pale
pink slips were compulsory
for field trips, to skip the shower
after gym class, escape school
for a dental appointment or worse,
because a father died.

And now a mother's long dead
too, her pink consent to speak
about her firstborn daughter
unnecessary, the one she left
for adoption in California
where she hid three seasons
before returning to Iowa.

Who harbored her there?
Was it consensual?
Did she know the father?
Why couldn't she tell you?

I sing like a canary, spill
her secret beans, travel twelve
hundred miles to meet my half
sister, who does not need clearance
to be gay, a recovering addict.
We sit close, comparing
the labyrinths of our hands.

Scenes from Easter Sunday 1982
Stephanie Axley-Cordial

My stepmother has given me braids
That are too weak to hold the style on their own.
She attacks my hair with the spray that makes my eyeballs and throat sticky.

I'm wearing the white cotton dress with thin multicolored ribbons
weaving through the eyelet lace, binding my diaphragm from an audible inhale,
tights that never reach the top, and shoes I cannot fill that leave blisters on my heels.

I try to focus on the comforting dotted yellow lines on the highway
while my dad and stepmother chain smoke family secrets
in whispers from the front seat.

Grandpa, the head and me, a stool at the corner of the far end.
Empty promises are piled on my plate.
I am starving, I do not have enough room to cut my ham.

Someone opens a bottle of wine slurring nothings in an exaggerated French accent.
Disappointments trickle down to me in the form of untold stories and offerings of gum.
The table is littered with dessert plates and interrupted small talk.

I sneak up to bed, not wanting to show everyone how I look in the nightgown Aunt Pam
got me.
Tomorrow my hair will be too much to do anything, my throat too
hoarse from the residue of everyone else's expectations to even speak.

Pizza Party
Erin Jamieson

The pizza was more grease than cheese or sauce, leaving oily residue on my hands. Your birthday party, one of the many I attended simply because I was young. There was pepperoni pizza two, and garlic breadsticks that felt like pillows in my mouth.

Mom served the cake: thick, sapphire blue icing, though I don't remember the theme. it was cloying sweet, a forced celebration sliding down my throat.

In birthdays past, you might have looked at me, asked if I was getting cake too.

This was the first time you didn't, the first time you were ashamed to have your little sister there, and maybe the last of your parties Mom brought me too.

I was relieved at first. I didn't like feeling like a side decoration. I didn't want to worry about your friends. But every once in a while, I see a decorated cake in a store and think of that moment.

The Gift
Rich Orloff

In the middle of the night
In total darkness
When I was very young
The people who surrounded me offered me the gift of shame

It will solve your problems, they told me
It will ease your pain
It will comfort you when you feel alone
It will make you one of us

I took a bite
It was bitter
Swallow, they insisted
So I did

As long as you make this part of your diet, they said
We will embrace you
And if I don't, I asked
You will die alone, they replied simply

That's how shame became part of my regular diet
Until it felt so integral
I was addicted
And sometimes even enjoyed the high

Withdrawal can be excruciating
And love can feel so scarce
So if you see me return to shame at times
Just know that every now and then I need to rest in the familiar

Pom Pom Pull Away
Barbara Meier

Taupe gray twigs hanging by a strip of brown bark, from the branches of a Chinese Elm,
like graphite lead applied to the skies, a fat pencil held by curly fingernails on a Big Chief
tablet, from elm trees with disease, now dead.

The first Chinese elm tree was a house we played in,
the bent trunk forming a table with mottled leaves for cups,
spent twigs for teaspoons, and a branch to sweep the fine dust away.

The second Chinese elm was a jungle gym to climb
and swing like Tarzan on a thin bark line.

The third, a fort to hide behind banks of snow,
winging snowballs at boys in red plaid jackets and caps with flaps.

A fourth a bench to watch the horses graze behind barbed wire fences.
Tails and manes flicking flies away from eyes, coats glistening
in a sheen of warm sunlight, memories stored on the eyelashes and velvet eyes.

Sixty years ago we played around the trees at our school, eating wild onions in the field,
picking purple poppy mallow flowers to tuck behind our ears. Shrieking, feinting,
playing pom pom pullaway, never wanting to be IT.

Little girls who grew up and died.
Farm boys who still harvest the wheat.
A third-grade boy whose lips stuck to the outdoor water fountain.
The first-grade boy who licked the stick from his paste jar.

Children who moved away to big cities, barely remembering
the Farmers Elevator and the elevator man who gave out sticks of gum,
or the Union Pacific train gliding on ghost rails carrying
the cream, butter, and eggs to Salina.
All the little ones who lived and played on the prairie,
Who will remember them now?
I will scratch the sky with words and names and stir up the dead leaves with my breath,
placing them between the pages of thick books, hoping someone will find them on some
shelf somewhere to marvel and wonder at what used to be.

*Pom Pom Pull Away: Children line up as in Red Rover. One child stays in the center
and says, "Pom Pom Pull Away". With this the children run to the other side. If a child is
tagged, he/she must stay in the middle to help tag others. The first child tagged is 'it' for
the next game.

Moved (Emma)
Mauro Altamura

Emma pushed her palsied legs hard, terribly hard, on the pedals, dying to get her bike to move over the riverside walkway. She just wanted a little distance. That was all.

"Come on, Emma. You want to move? Then try harder." Dad shouted from twenty feet away, easy, straddled over his bright orange Trek. He was on the phone, of course. "What's the problem?"

Why the yelling, Dad? In front of everyone, no less. Bad enough that at thirteen she had to use training wheels. He's inhuman, Emma had decided long ago. She watched his calves and thigh muscles knit tight like the twisty braids he'd told her he loved when he spotted them on other teenage girls, her few friends included.

"Hard, Em. Like stepping on a bug." Dad pressed his right foot into the pavers.

She pushed down again, sure she felt a forehead vein bulge thick as an earthworm under her pink safety helmet, felt it pulse electrically, blood coursing around her brain.

Other walkers, runners, bikers – normals all – turned their heads. She stayed put in the middle of the path. Some stopped for selfies, the Statue of Liberty over their shoulders. Emma would bet anything they were really staring at her and her wormy forehead.

"Look at that," a random grandma said to her granddaughter. "You can touch Lady Liberty if you reach out." Granny pointed while the girl, also on a trike, but about five, giggled, reached out. Skinny, perfect fingers tickled the air. "Keep going, sweetie. You'll touch her."

Sure, touch her. Lousy kid. Emma tried hard just to keep her spazzy arms straight, barely able to wrap her fingers around the handlebar grips, around anything. She pressed her palms hard into the bike's dirty white plastic grips, as if that would ever help her go.

Grandma and the girl left. Good riddance. Who needed to see some special little giggler and the dumb Granny fawning? Emma tried both feet on the pedals, the left higher than the right. She imagined the downward thrust of her left leg was super fierce, so strong she could kick through someone's ribs if she wanted. As if! The pressure did nothing. Only caused her butt to raise, her shoulders to jut forward, maybe a forty-five degree angle.

Emma looked up. Dad had wandered off, now really shouting into his phone, the words lost in the wind. She tried to catch his eye, get his attention. No response. Did he even freaking see her? She still couldn't straighten up, though maybe got to a little more than the forty-five degrees. She remembered the protractor Ms. Famigletti had used in fourth grade to show them how to measure angles, positioning kids so their bodies would mimic lines. She'd watch as her classmates stood straight, bent easily.

"You'll never stand a straight ninety," stupid Paulie Williams had said to her. Well. Asshole got left back in fourth grade and had to go to Catholic when he didn't get promoted in fifth, either. Paulie and the rest of Emma's past hung around, sticky and annoying. She hadn't laughed when she saw his pathetic baby tears drip after he learned he'd been left back. Served him right, though. Him and Charlie Finnerty both kept back that year. Poor Charlie stuttered like a cicada, unable to read a full sentence without his face going red. He wasn't a jerk like Paulie, wasn't dumb, either. The school kept him back only because they didn't want to deal with getting him help.

"Emma's ok. She can keep moving," the principal had told Dad.

"Moving?" Dad said. "Really?"

*

Emma stood a little higher when she pressed again. Maybe fifty degrees now, by a protractor's measure. The big wood half-moon instrument seemed to float right next to her. Emma remembered its flat bottom helped the others draw straight lines on the white board. Not her. She could barely hold a marker, errant lines shooting all over the board's slick surface. Thank god so few watched her during Math, had their ears and lips snuck into phones, or flirting, kids already paired up. Her? No one said boo. She remembered sending Jackie Sola a birthday card. A Friday, right before winter break. Kids couldn't wait to get out. They'd had enough of math and social sciences, enough of the lunchroom's stale pizza. Enough angles. She watched Jackie open, then stuff the card in his History book. At least he didn't tear it up – at least not in front of her.

"Thatta girl, Em. You're getting there." Still on his cell, Dad glanced her way, took a few steps closer.

How nice of you to say, Dad!

His face smushed back into the phone. "Listen, I am not helping," he said. "You left us."

Emma curled her lips and nose and hoped he saw. He was talking to Mom again, Big Em, trying once more to get back in their lives. Dad, jerk. Mom, forget, way out in New Mexico, running ayahuasca groups, leading other fifty-somethings through their psychedelic trips, promising bliss or revelation, maybe escape from whatever crappy family they'd also run away from. Emma's shrink told her not to stay in the bad space re Mom, where things were eff-ed up, where life eff-ing sucked.

"No, Emma," Shrink Rebecca said. "You've gone past that. You've walked through that space and away."

"Walked through," Emma would mutter. "Right." As if. More like stumbled. Crawled? I'm in that space where I crawl, she thought. Ugh. Space. Emma hated when she heard people use the word like that. Space is wide open land, or what's beyond earth's atmosphere. Maybe a closet. People had lots of space, closet and otherwise, if they were rich or could move from shit hole Jersey City to somewhere like New Mexico. Mom had sent two pictures a few years ago. One of her walk-in, with pink and orange dresses strewn over hangers. The other a view from her backyard, which looked as big as a park. 'Lots of space out here,' Mom wrote. Emma thought at first she'd tear the pix up, but decided to hide them in her underwear drawer. Once in a while she looked. Like Mom's dresses, the cacti's budding flowers were also pink and orange. Weird. The photos were the only things she had from Mom after she'd abandoned her and Dad. Freaked out, Dad had said.

"Too many problems for your mother, and, bam, gone." Dad threw every possession of Big Em's into the garbage. He didn't know about the pictures, otherwise they'd be gone, too. That was all she had, besides the name. And though it was kind of gross – Emmuh, as she pronounced it, syllables elided, the last sound muffled as if she were about to barf – she actually loved her name. She'd looked it up early, found it meant whole. In Hebrew, 'all containing.' Really? That was bullshit. Though she'd been Bat Mitzvahed and was absolutely a Jew, she definitely wasn't all containing, considering her limitations. Her disability. Her self. Emma knew the reason for the crap body, too, learned the whole story after Big Em split and finally sent a fifteen page letter revealing not only that she and Dad were freaking forty when Em was born, (no kidding, Mom. Math!) but they'd done enough acid over the years to wreck their chromosomes and ensure they'd have flashbacks for the rest of their lives. Zero info about why she'd left, why she didn't care enough to stay and help. Emma burned the letter on the stove immediately, happy they hadn't had another kid, another crip like her. One was enough. Age and acid didn't make for healthy children.

*

"Where are you now?" Dad shouted.

For a second Emma thought, WTF? I'm right here, dipshit. Twenty feet away. But she realized he was still talking with Mom. Still! At least not with one of his business deals, real estate or property development, whatever he did, all that space he had to rent or sell. Dad turned some, but didn't face her. He was so damn healthy, so well tuned, all muscled and in-place hair. Emma definitely not, not one bit. Hair scraggly, face smudged with leftover food, dirt under the fingernails. She'd only get really clean when she soaked in the tub for an hour, the quiet luxury she loved to take, the sweetness she gave herself, the way Mom did (must have done?) for her. Then she'd feel relaxed, feel perfect. Pure, dirt free. She'd make the water steaming hot like Mom probably did. Step in, let the luscious water dissolve the crud, float it off her body. Her skin soon red. The particles and grit would form an iridescent sheen around her chest and crooked legs, as if her disease had leeched out, disappearing into the water's knife-thin surface. In that hour, nothing is wrong. Nothing can touch her.

Ultimately, though, the water turns cold, turns on her like everything else. And the worst thing ever? Dad has to help her out, has to see her covered with the towel that's gotten soaked and clings tight to her body, her boobs little, but there. Coming. She hopes they will. She covers them, unsure what to do. What to reveal.

"Just help me stand, Dad," she will say. "And look away. Just... please."

He does. He listens to that. She believes he actually doesn't want to look at her. Maybe can't.

Just that once, though, she did see his face go red, and yes, for sure, he'd cried.

*

"So where the hell are you?" Dad shouted again. "Is anyone helping?" He turned again, face to the statue, to the patina of Liberty, the green of Liberty, the crown of the statue woman with her strong arm stretched, a brilliant torch that fooled people into the belief they'd be welcomed and cared for. Lady Liberty. Really?

"Jail? And no one's helping you? Oh, Em, Em. Why're you doing this? Why still with this stupid ayahuasca? Didn't you trip enough? Didn't we do enough shit when we were young?" Dad turned fast. He faced Emma, scrunched his face more. Mom was begging for help, again. Begging to come home, again. Dad wouldn't have it, as always.

Emma watched for a long minute. Poor Dad's face contorted, and in that instant an electric bolt, a beam of light shot between them, Dad to her, her to Dad, their brains, their psyches, maybe their souls, if they had any. Their eyes locked, a pipeline right to each other in an immediate blast of recognition.

Dad's bolt said: Big Em's too far gone this time, kid. She's over for us. Finally. Gone for good.

Emma's bolt said: I'm done and gone, too. Enough from Big Em, enough trying to connect to her. She left, not me. She's the so-called mother. Joke, right? Come to think of it, enough from you, Dad, too. Done with you, this crappy day, this crappy body. Enough of it all.

Emma stopped listening to his conversation, words no longer making sense. She watched his face squeeze, squeeze, vanish. His voice, Big Em's voice, poof, disappeared.

She looked at the lousy statue. None of the stories were true, but at least it got people to try. So maybe she could ride. Emma pressed her left foot with all her strength. The pedal went down. She pressed the right one. Down it went, too. The left again and then the right. Repeat, repeat. The wheels moved. Front, back, trainers, the whole damn bike. Forward. She, the bike, they moved. All by herself. Moved.

Conversatin'
Lindsey Morrison Grant

Puke
Autumn Zevallos

✧   In Middle School
I caught an episode of *1000 Ways To Die*
one afternoon;
in it, a model had died
from rupturing
the lining of her stomach.

Slowly,
everything she meant
to empty out into that porcelain bowl
poured out instead
inside of her.

✧   In 10th grade
I dated a girl who always disappeared
after she ate,
without a word
of where she went,
but a locked bathroom door
could not stop the secrets
from seeping through the cracks.

Then I was alone,
guided only by
the grooves in the dirt;
following the footfalls
of a phantom.
She looked back one last time,
words of warning etched in her gaze,
this will hurt
and I cannot watch.

✧   In 11th grade
      I was noticed,
complemented, for the
first time for the
      way I was able to waste
      away.

Celebrated
for separating myself,
fifty pounds apart from
      from the stranger I was

last year.

✧   In 12th grade
       Christine cried when I told her
       I was to be sent to Wisconsin
       because the doctors said
       I was dying, and desperately
       in need of treatment,
       with no hospital close to home
            that would take me.

       In the end,
       I did not go
       for I feared the weight
       of her tears far more
       than a staggering
       mortality rate.
       In fact, in the face
       of the odds,
I felt nothing.
       If it would end,
       it would end.

✧   In the ten years since
       It did not end.
       I did not end, but
       I have died,
       again and again
       in a cycle I thought
            never ending;

            head slumped in prayer
            or exhaustion,
            coming to learn
            through these cycles of rebirth
            that the only being
            that needed to hear my pleas
            was me.

The Boy in the Puddle
Patrick Geraghty

PART I - The Man in the Doorway

Tommy remembered when he was a little kid, about 6-7 years old, and was afraid to sleep because of the silhouette of a man in the doorway, and the man was there in the daytime too. Something about it scared the boy deep down.

The boy stared at his doorway. If it were open, whenever he closed his eyes, he knew the silhouette would be there when he opened his eyes again. But it was worse when the door was closed because the man in the doorway could be standing just the other side of the door, about to kick his leg through it and bust it down, or so the boy imagined. Maybe the boy could see the shadows of the man's feet as he stood on the other side of the doorway. The boy stared. So, he didn't sleep, and slept little when he did fall asleep at all.

He thought about it much later. When did it start? He had no idea. That was buried deeply, and it lay quietly, or so he thought. Because, of course, there was, in fact, a man in the doorway, long ago, and the man was the boy's abuser. And that man was the boy's father.

He never thought about it anymore, how his dad would sit next to him as he lay on the bed, or how they would bathe together when he was little. Those were terrible times and the only awareness he carried was the silhouette of the man in the doorway.

Because the man did not stay in the doorway. Not for long. And not even the first time either. He came in every time and it was inevitable what happened from there. What's a 5-year-old boy to do? Take it. Just take it. And at some point it would stop. He could endure anything. He proved that to himself time and time again. There was always a moment when the man was done, and then the heavy mass climbed off and scampered out. Like a cockroach. Gone.

But he'd be back.

By day, he was a cranky, absent father. But some nights he was a terrible grunting hulk--a huge heavy bag of skin. The boy never had a close friend because he had a huge secret he couldn't share. Later, he was told his dad violated all his childhood boundaries, so he grew up with no boundaries at all, and tried to please everyone. Which was true. He was a people-pleaser and a liar, and eventually, a drunk. But that came later. Long ago, he was a little kid and he'd just try to make it through the night.

Now he remembered if they went out to dinner with his father, the boy would get so sick he'd have to wait in the car. That happened every time. But somehow, no one put it together. His mother must have at least noticed there was no one in bed with her at night, so her husband had to be somewhere else. Did it ever occur to her where he was and what he was doing? It's hard to believe it didn't, but she didn't intervene, and that's a fact, he thought. Or she wouldn't let herself acknowledge her part in an awful, incestuous, family of four.

What about his little brother? Did their father get him too? He had no idea. He was too focused on himself to worry about anyone else, but his brother is much older now, and morbidly obese. So, his therapist says, he's probably a victim too.

Tommy's told he is called a survivor. That sounds close to the truth. He's alive now, but just barely. He doesn't ever feel emotions, and eventually an ex-girlfriend complained because of a complete lack affection. But how could he tell her that touching, to him, was a bad thing, because it led to worse things? How could he tell her that sex made him feel horrible and dirty and shameful? Shame. He carried a lot of shame. And its deep within him.

So he carried this burden and soldiered forward without any thought. He believed he was content to spend my life suffering under the shadow of something that happened when he was 4 or 5 years old, and a few years later, big enough to fight him off. He remembered the day he surprised the fucker, and the boy fought at him, and his father was no match for the boy's vehemence. He had a lot of rage stored away. He still does.

Sometimes when he's sitting alone his mind drifts and, before he knows it, he's back in the dark room again with the suffocating heap on top of him. Its terrifically hot and sticky. He closes his eyes and takes himself away to anywhere. And it works because it's over before he thinks about it.

And then he was hiding behind a door to the kitchen. His father was drunk and passed out in there. *Can't you Hear Me Knockin by* the Stones played on the radio.

The boy could hear his slow, ragged breathing as he sat in the kitchen with his head resting on his arms. The empty bottle of rye sat against his elbow. The boy knew the man was passed out, probably for the night. He crept slowly passed him and went to the butcher block. On there was a sharp paring knife. The boy felt the blade with his thumb. Careful, it was really sharp and drew blood from his finger. He sucked his thumb and gripped the knife tightly in his other hand, as if the man would get up and wrestle him for it. Slowly, oh so slowly, he crept toward the man and found a place where his neck was exposed. The boy pressed the blade against the man's neck until a thin line of blood opened up.

And that's as far as he got, and the silhouette remained, etched into his life.

PART II - *The Puddle*

Alone in the house one day, his babysitter sat next to him on the couch in the family room. "Smell my hair," she whispered and skootched her 13-year-old body next to his 7-year-old one. Tommy shook and shrank back from her. She ran her fingers thru her long brown hair. "C'mon," she said, I have a new shampoo," and Tommy staggered off the couch and out of the family room. He sat in the living room and shivered.

He could hear Julie laugh in the other room. "C'mon Tommy, don't be so shy" she sang, but Tommy wasn't shy, he was scared. He didn't know what she wanted from him. She was taller than him and she had boobs. Tommy was small and skinny and weak.

"Let's go downstairs, "she said as she walked toward the basement door. "C'mon Tommy."

He calmed a bit and found himself walking toward the door then down the steps.

"Wanta drink?" She giggled from behind his dad's bar down there. "Sure'" he said as he sat on a barstool across from her. She poured him a club soda and mixed it with some orange juice from the mini fridge under the bar . Here you go, that'll be $3 she said, but Tommy only had a dollar.

"C'mon, pretend." she said, so he explored his pockets and counted out the imaginary bills. He drank some and she finished it.

"Want another?" She asked. "Sure" he said, and this time she poured something creamy and tan from a brown bottle that looked like a light bulb. It smelled like sweet gasoline. "Try this." She said.

He took a big swallow, and then he heard underwater sounds and then the hanging lights above the bar swayed a little and he was all right, and then he was good, no great. He finished the glass.

He looked up and smiled at her. "C'mon, let's play pinball," he said as he hopped from the barstool to the floor. She followed him and held his hand and he squeezed hers.

"You first," he said, confident now. She played and he leaned over the side of the glass and watched her ball ping around the machine, her flippers flapping.

He went back to the bar for some more. "Want some?" he asked filling the glass. "It's good."

"Sure," she said and took a tentative sip. He took the cup from her and took a huge gulp. It was thick and sweet and he loved it. He started to giggle and then laugh as he hopped from the bar and over to the pool table, totally energized now. "Let's play," he said. She poured more, took a quick sip and said "Sure!" and he racked the balls and broke them the way he'd seen his father do it so many times. It was easy now. He handed the stick to her. "Your turn." Her hand touched his and he didn't care. He had no fear. He thought about school and the girls there and how he would talk with them when he got there tomorrow and how they'd like him, and the boys too. He jumped up and down in place and laughed wildly, as happy as he could remember being. "Let's go outside!" he laughed, and he held her hand and led her up the stairs and out the back door. "What do you want to do?" She asked. "I don't know," he said twirling in place. Let's go to the store."

So they walked through the gate to the front and onto the sidewalk toward the store that was a few blocks away. But Tommy couldn't stay on the sidewalk. He was too happy and hyper, and he found himself up on the lawns where he smelled the yellow flowers that grew there by the houses, and then he was back on the sidewalk next to his babysitter laughing wildly. He grabbed her hand and skipped down the sidewalk to the store as he sang *Satisfaction* by the Stones as loud as he could.

"You wait outside," she said to him firmly, but he laughed and walked into the store. "What should we get?" he said loudly. "Let's get some gum." And he had a dollar so he gave it to the man and took the gum and went outside and waited for Julie who came out a few minutes later with a soda. Tommy flipped a piece of gum in his mouth and grabbed the soda and took a long gulp, but the soda foamed out of his mouth and down the front of his shirt and he didn't care.

"C'mon Tommy," we ought to get home," she said, and she grabbed his hand a tugged it toward the sidewalk and he followed her while walking from side to side so he twisted her around as they walked.

He was having the best time of his life.

He ran the rest of the way home and into the door and then downstairs for some more. He laughed wildly and started to play pinball. She came downstairs and he grabbed her around the waist and he put his nose in her hair and breathed deeply.

"See," she whispered, "It smells like apples."

Last day of school before winter break
Susan Kolon

The box is wrapped in virgin white tissue,
lipstick-red ribbon trailing on top. Here,
he says, Merry Christmas! handing it to me
as I hop off the bus. He rears his chin,
tosses his hair back into place and runs

toward a group of boys swirled in smirks
and shouts, doesn't look back. Leaves me
standing in the swoon of holding hands
at the movies, roller skating, Nerfball.
The gift in my grip, proof he likes me back.

In the pink-walled solitude of my bedroom,
clusters of jade whisper to me, and I am
as bright and alive as the crimson ribbon
that contains the promise of a daring me.
Who will not watch from shore next summer

as waves roll the brave girls into its coil,
catching the eye of laughing boys who swim
nearby. On the gift tag is the name
I have secreted into notebooks. I want
this gift unwrapped. Protecting the layers,

I leave no rips, no tears. Inside,
a dog bone. Dull brown and bowed.
The slow creep of my shame places the box
under a canopy bed, a wreathed screen
of dark, shadowed by gloating paper.

Until Christmas Day. On its maiden voyage,
I fly to boy's house on the sparkled banana
seat of my gold and purple bicycle, deck
the box onto his front lawn. There. I am
a bright color after all.

Medio oeste
Olivia Muñoz

On our new land: The honors and accolades that hold up a wall in my parents' house in little Saginaw, Michigan. My dad's love of Motown music. Boots heavy with dirt from Midwestern beet fields. A box of corn tortillas, pig intestines, a block of cheese brought an hour and a half north from Detroit, where there are more of us, enough of us to form Mexicantown, right there, overlooking Canada. A stone tub hauled up from Mexico and my godfather's heavy hand. The 21-year-old birth certificate of some stranger clutched in my 58-year-old aunt's hand as we cross the border from there to there. Prayers whispered up to the Blind Souls. My 10-year-old braids offered to the Virgin Mary in exchange for the eradication of these headaches. The weight of my accent as it flutters away from me after years of college. Getting off welfare.

Breasts At a Moment During a Threesome at 16
Billie Sainwood

First there's the dark
blue and purple overlapping,
pressing together until black.
It looks like the entire world is a bruise
or like memory has swallowed all sight
or like the power is out at the Double Tree
where I have agreed to meet a married couple
for a threesome.

Then my eyes adjust
and I am sixteen, still a boy,
still closeted and shy.
The power is still out
and we are all silhouettes.

The husband, balding but in a cool way,
his chest, seabed smooth except for a kelp of hair.
His wife, glasses, nose ring, soft.
They ask me to take off my shirt
and my chubby, teen body blooms
in the dark like fragrant jasmine.
I am not quite the young stud from the pictures.
But I will do.

The husband becomes a director,
a starving man with a menu.
Commanded, the wife and I embrace
and our chests press together
melt together
like white chocolate in unskilled summertime hands.

In bed,
directed, I slip into her and try not to hope
she notices the difference
she can somehow detect the uncertainty
the tender bulb of woman in the thorns of all this.
I try not to hope she sees the wish in me
to be her
to be soft and splendid.

We rock together. He watches.
He smiles. He gleams like a wound in the dark.
He says things he's heard in porn.

He calls attention to his cock.
We rock and our breasts
are melting hourglasses
are molten geometry
are shared.

He steps towards us, hanging
next to our heads like a stage light.
"God, babe, your tits look so good."

First, there's the dark,
the barely visible of everything
like the power is out
like the memory wants to be uncertain
and painted over with the hopeful lie of looking back
of making dim eye contact with this woman
of sharing a private eye roll
of laughing under our performative moans.

Before transition.
Before coming out.
Before the signs.
Before I told anyone.

First, there was the dark
and the white knuckle hope
that I remember this right
that we laughed between moans
just between us girls
a little secret
about the man in the room.

Family History
Melissa Folini

My sister died with dreams,
unfinished college courses and business plans.
My Father lived with survivor guilt
until he too was taken.
Not the first but not the last, in a circle most decidedly vicious.
My Mother died too soon
but just in time
robbed of her dignity, her joy of food, and her taste for life.
I'm still here in the house they left long before their time,
living with their things, memories, my dreams, and unfulfilled legacies.

April Showers
Danielle Shandiin Emerson

Shiyazhí,   what will you   keep?
in the timber regions. July heat,
Ya'iishjááshtsoh, orange and yellow blubs
heavy-lidded eyes, pressed inward with my   palms.
rocks in my spine, tether my loose body to the ground and
build like stacked pieces of   river rocks.
Bundles of ch'ilgohwehih, collected in plastic Walmart bags,
hung like bracelets along my cousin's wrists
Picked, plucked, pulled on the side of the   old highway,
where accidents seemed predetermined.
 I feel lost, unsure
wholá, turning over dirt in my hands.
Weeds graze my knees, as I step into the sky, where specs of
shandiin   falls on sun-loved skin.   My cousin walks with her back
tall, strong like Navajo Tea, growing in front of bluffs,
I feel like crying, collapsing.
 But shiyazhí, you say, watch the stars rise again,   night
after night. They look like your sibling's eyes, bright,   bright
and when people ask, what will you keep?
With bunches of Navajo Tea in my hands—clasped tight,
chil'go dootł'izh staining my fingers.
I'll keep their love,
      my cousin's strength, stems of ch'ilgohwehih refusing to bend
         as cars drive by disturbing a budding nizhoní-ful
 silence.

Unfinished Business
Lee Pendergrass

a baby
box rests
in the corner   blue
and white stripes fall
down its angled edges

the box is full
of little things:
a travel bottle
of unscented lotion, a pack of
baby
wipes, a thick-paged book
about shapes, an unopened
pacifier, a small stack of
newborn
diapers, a hand-knit
beanie, an otter onesie saying

"welcome to the world"

heavy with Day 1 things,
the baby box restlessly waits,
still
shelved at Day 237
past due.

Unfinished
Tom Russell

"Nine-one-one, what is your emergency?"

"I just killed my baby," she said. Her voice sounded so soft and calm. Not maniacal or hysterical. Not in any way evil. Not in any way anything. My inner voice was pleading, "No. Please, no!" I answered her in a voice as cool and calm as her own, asking, "Where are you?" This was in the mid-1980s before we got the enhanced 911 features that display the caller's location on a computer screen. I don't know why she didn't tell me where she was. Another dispatcher picked up the line to listen in. His job was to start an emergency response once we knew where she was while I kept her talking on the line. He called the chief operator at the telephone company to have the call traced. It took a few minutes to get that information.

Meanwhile, I remained on the line, talking in a comforting voice. She'd be gone if she heard the wrong words or got a bad vibe. It felt like trying to disarm a bomb that was steadily ticking away. We remained tethered while my partner got the address from the chief operator and sent a fire engine and ambulance to her location. A police dispatcher sent a couple of officers and a sergeant there. When they arrived, I told her someone was there to help her and asked her to please meet them at the door. She went to let them in.

After a short while, the officer working the case called the police dispatcher on the phone instead of the radio and said, "We're going to need a coroner here." Because of scanners, we had a "home listening audience." But they couldn't hear our phone conversations, so the officer kept it discreet instead of broadcasting the death to whoever was listening.

Usually, there was plenty of talking going on in the communications room. A lot of coordination between agencies or departments that we facilitated and dispatchers talking about calls that we received. But when we heard the police dispatcher tell the sheriff's dispatcher that the officers on the scene needed a coroner, it got pretty quiet for just a bit. I had mixed emotions about this. I couldn't immediately understand why a mother would kill her infant. She carried that baby around for all those months and put up with things that made pregnancy difficult. And then she killed him. I was sad about the baby and angry with the mother who had drowned the boy while bathing him.

I needed a reasonable explanation for such a nightmare. Could there be one? Maybe she couldn't help herself because of an illness. The chaotic battle with hormones and depression might have led to postpartum psychosis. I've read that the casualties of this type of trauma might lose track of reality as it brings on hallucinations, delusions, mood swings, and behavior changes. Yeah, that must have been it.

It's difficult to recall what came out at her trial. It's also hard to imagine that she was found guilty of anything, but I wasn't there. We often didn't get the final disposition of the calls we took. You handle one emergency and move on to the next one. By the time the verdict came out, most of us were probably not reliving that day and had taken hundreds of calls since then.

Sometimes, officers would come into the 911 center and tell us about some of the calls we'd sent them on and show pictures of the scene. They also wanted to know what was said on the phone so they could include it in their reports.

Some Saturday mornings, after working all Friday night, cops and dispatchers met at a bar to talk shop over beers. We learned about some of the calls and the people involved in them. There were many repeat offenders and stories to go with each one.

At the trial, they probably played the recording of the call the mother made to 911 after her son's death. Everything said on the radio or in a phone call was recorded on a large reel-to-reel tape recorder. I once had to testify at a murder trial where the recording of what happened in that case was instrumental in convicting the shooter.

We always discussed the incoming calls and how we were handling them. Then, the discussion was interrupted by more work. Many conversations went unfinished in that room. There were ghosts of those conversations floating in the clouds of cigarette smoke that blanketed the basement chamber. Medical emergencies, domestic disturbances, and mental health crises cut them off. One caller said his neighbor was standing on the roof of his own house shouting that the Intergalactic Ku Klux Klan had just landed there and that he, the neighbor, needed an "immediate interrogation." All you can do is use your brain, training, and experience to react calmly and appropriately.

That baby boy never got to take his first step or tell his mother he loved her. She will never forget that. I can barely imagine the vivid colors of horror she saw while standing alone in her house after drowning him. She had no one to talk to until she made the 911 call. She and I bonded that day, in that moment. I still wonder if she was able to truly connect with anyone after that tragedy, or is she still alone, floating in a cold, dark oblivion, never to be reeled in. Where are you?

Cold pizza in bed
Danielle McMahon

This is what a sore thumb looks like
a stray hangnail thumping redly
like the jagged husk of a pizzacrust
kicked and gutted piles of bedding loosed
and endless fluff it's all too much to consider even a trip
to the stairs a flight of shuffling heavy feet overheard *and oh*
won't someone bring me more cold pizza in bed and
filmy dietsodapop to ease this acrid soulpit

This is what the baby blues looks like the
postbabyblues the grownbabyblues *dear lord the no-*
babyblues a hollow kind of wasting greased-
with-sweat-pants stains slung around slack hips and
blooms of purple bruising like a faded photograph an
old phonograph a faraway voice haughty and
mewling on about *love love hopelesslove* and that
is what you get echoing inside of your head or maybe
it's your heart licking away at the wound of time *and you know it is*
what it is whatitis what-it-is darling a shame a terribleterrible shame

This is what grief looks like *ho ho! ha ha!*
a stubborn rooting to the wreckage cold hands
opening like useless candelabras like
hands cupping dirty dishes fluttering with bruises all
plattered up and all of it purple
purplepurplepurple the endless contusive clanging *and besides*
he did not mean it and besides
it had been a bad day

Bedside,

you can feel the incoming phonecall the voice preaching
you gottagottagotta get up mother said you ought to get out
of bed your daddy your dear old daddy is deadstonedead but when does it
end and where do you take it this sick sad song of grief this bed
a hovel your hollow protests an empty verse to gurgle into
wet socks cryaching jaw jagged stale crumbs in the creases

of your wearied eyes do you fold it up neatly into a pizzabox
tuck it in and away? plate it up potluck paperstyle to serve deadly cold?
I have an inkling for you you have to *kill it killit kill it in its crib*

The Next Fossil II
Timothy Dodd

After my youth was done, I stumbled out of the forest,
off the mountain, onto the hot blacktop of the filling
station. I walked up in a daze to one of the six gasoline
pumps, lifted the handle from its dispenser and placed
the aluminum nozzle inside my mouth like a suicide.
I squeezed the trigger and fired shot into the throat,
down into stomach, deep into my body, molding me
into wet tar. I climbed back into the hills, hardening
overnight into sedimentary rock, then waited watched
until heat, pressure, time, and microbes transformed me
into an energy they could burn, at some point no longer
worried that all the trees and flowers were left for dead.

Stages of Grief
Stone

1 I do not feel like a rape victim. I call a trauma counselor because that is what a rape victim should do. That is what feels like the correct course of action, an autopilot response. When I step into her office she doesn't treat me like a rape victim because I don't act like a rape victim because I don't feel like a rape victim. The first time I leave the office I see quotes on the wall about survival and do not relate because I didn't survive it.

3. I go to the Walgreens across the street and sit on the linoleum floor in the fluorescent lighting looking at nail polish. All in all, I spend over a grand on bright reds, vivid blues, every color I can imagine. As the cashier bags them and the glasses of varnish clink against other cacaphonically, I remember the way he had told me how much he liked the color I painted my nails that night and I convince myself that if I choose the right color, this will never happen again.

2. I lie awake every night concocting plans of how to kill him. I try to think of a way that won't leave me legally culpable because the law had already failed me in this situation. I think of a tragic accident where I loosen the guardrails by the aquarium and he falls into a vat of electric eels where he is as helpless as I was. In these fantasies, I wonder if the eels are more kind than he was to me, and I'm sure they are.

4 When I'm calling out sick from work I don't know how to put into words that everything feels like an explosion and vacuum all at once. I don't know how to tell them that leaving my bed in the morning is the hardest thing I've ever done, but staying in bed all day is also the hardest thing I've ever done. That brushing my teeth, putting on a bra, looking at my own face in the mirror are all marathons of effort that I don't have the stamina for anymore, so no Stephanie at JCPenney, I can't come in to work to sell jeans because I have to relearn how to breathe. She tells me to get my act together. I tell her I know. I try to find the number to the trauma counselor again, but two phone calls in one day is too much work so I just go back to sleep.

1 i tell my mom that everything is fine, that my relationship is great, and that my boyfriend definitely isn't a rapist. I tell her it's a rough patch at worst. She believes me, and I almost do too.

2. When I find the number for the trauma counselor again she encourages me to start working out when I start to get angry to be more productive with it. Between the protein shakes and fits of rage, I get like, fucking jacked. I don't feel better but I do look cooler. I get furious that I live in the reality where I have muscles instead of the one where I didn't get raped. The anger leads to another workout, which leads to more muscles, which leads to more anger.

4 I start antidepressants and they made me throw up every hour for 5 days straight. I get an ulcer from the stress but at least I am not depressed anymore.

5. 5 years, when someone at the open mic reads a poem about rape, I do not immediately cry. I ask my therapist if this means I'm healing. He asks if I still feel like a rape victim. I have to hesitate to think about when I started feeling like one versus when I stopped. I don't have an answer for either. I still ask if this is healing. Where do we draw the line of coping, healing, forgetting, repressing? Was I healed when I first stepped into that trauma office, and accepted that I did not survive what he did to me?

1 I do not feel like a rape victim.

Father
Mauro Altamura

I never noticed any gray in Father's hair, not until I saw him in his coffin. Certainly not years earlier, when I was eight, the first time he raped me. It occurred in the basement while Mother was at a card party sponsored by St. Joseph's Women's Auxiliary. Michael, my six-year-old brother, was wheezing in his sleep in our bedroom. The facts of the event are blurred, though from others' stories I hear and read, my experience is similar. I do consider myself somewhat lucky: the rapes only lasted for a period of nine months.

Father worked as a carpenter, alone and independent. He generally built interior stairs for wealthy families who desired exquisite handcraft. In bad times he would take on most any kind of job involving wood that he could find. He was a tall man – very tall, he always seemed to me – though others might not agree. His hands were hard with calluses, and his smell strong without being offensive. His thick wavy hair was slicked back from his forehead. A tuft often came loose and fell down into his eyes. When this happened he cursed and fled to the bathroom to correct it. He precisely combed and carefully arranged his hair each day.

As a rule, we kept a respectful distance, Father and I, although he taught me to swim and play catch, and he participated with me in the Cub Scouts like other fathers. He spoke primarily when he needed to communicate some practical information, or to have me bring him a tool. Mother was the one who discussed my difficulty with schoolwork or fighting with classmates, my reluctance to play with my brother. Nothing more than that was ever brought up.

Mother seemed happy enough, and my parents set aside most every Saturday night for themselves. They went to a movie, or with friends to a dinner-dance, to what at the time was called an affair. Their sex life was normal, from all I could tell. I am aware in retrospect of a rhythmic beat, which originated in their room. The sound wafted through our home every Sunday, the cadence borne on the gray light of early morning. It was the only time they seemed to have intercourse, but they performed faithfully.

We lived in a small wood frame house in Asbury Park, New Jersey, not far from the ocean. Father mostly worked on homes near ours, and each seemed exactly the same in every respect. I often rode my bicycle to deliver him the sandwich and snack Mother prepared for his lunch. Other fathers went to work at factories, or in small businesses. Some drove trucks on distant routes. My father was always close by.

My brother Michael was freckled, red-haired and exceptionally thin. He suffered with asthma from birth, and his health caused constant worry to my parents, Father in particular. Any time Mikey took ill, Father paced in silence through our rooms while Mother tended to her son. Mikey's attacks often began innocently. We might be gathered around the kitchen table, waiting for the daily meals of meat, starch, and vegetable. Perhaps my brother had been laughing due to being tickled by Father. If he continued to laugh, Mikey would draw his shoulders around his neck, squeeze his eyes closed, and let out short coughs. Then he would wheeze and fight his own body to draw in air. Before long he was in bed while Mother hovered with tea and sugar. Father would arrive, sit in a straight-backed wood chair in the corner of the bedroom. Mother laid next to her young son as he strained. Father watched. He did not move when Mother brought more cups of tea and massaged Mikey's shoulders and back throughout the night. Hands in his lap, he tilted his head back and leaned on the wall behind the chair. I looked in to see Mikey, but only saw Father with his eyes closed, his lips slightly parted, his hair ordered on his head. He remained in that position for hours as Mother read a magazine, then dozed in the stillness. The windows were always unopened, for fear pollen, dust or other air-borne allergens might enter Mikey's lungs and initiate another attack. A darkened spot marked the wall where Father rested his head. For years I'd see it whenever I chose to look at the wall.

*

The rapes took place while I was in third grade. Our teacher, Sister Mary Vincent, was a young nun with a beet-red face, and a love for mathematics and, surprisingly, baseball. Televisions had been installed in our classrooms that summer. In early October the electronic buzz and excited play-by-play of the World Series filled the room instead of our afternoon lessons. Sister Vincent used statistics from the game to create math exercises, setting up problems on the board as the game played out. We kept pencil and paper ready at our desk, taking numerical notes to multiply balls and strikes, distances, and runs. She introduced us to averages, though most of the students had no idea how to compute this.

One day, as she was telling us how many hits Mickey Mantle would need to reach a .333 batting average, I asked her if the amount of hits necessary would change if he batted more often.

"Why should that matter?" Sister Vincent's beady eyes vibrated under her tightly knit brow.

I did not shrink in my seat, but answered with a rare show of confidence. "Well, the more times he is up, the more hits he'll have to get to make up for it." I had, in fact, grasped the concept.

"What if he gets less hits?" She held her index finger in the air, moving it in a wide circle. Her robes swirled, a miniature vortex of black.

"His average will go down." I did not see her, but only my words, which floated before me, an answer distinct from any human source.

Sister tossed a single piece of white chalk from one hand to the other. "Yes. Yes!" She pointed the chalk at me. "This boy," she said as she whirled around to the rest of the class, "is a genius." Each of my classmates' faces scrunched in jealousy at the pronouncement. I sat, a half-smile on my lips, their gaze on me.

Just before three o'clock Sister Vincent called me to her desk. "For your parents only." She licked the envelope's flap and handed it to me. The sun cast a diagonal shadow across the blackboard. The chalked math problems were barely visible in the dark half. The dismissal bell rang.

"Yes, Sister. Good afternoon."

"Good afternoon, what?"

"Good afternoon, Sister."

Father picked me up later, after my Cub Scout meeting. I gave him the envelope as soon as we were in the car. I leaned over his shoulder from the back seat as he slit it open and read. "Sit back in your seat." Father shielded the message with his shoulder. Before we started for home he looked at me and slid the note into his breast pocket. Father said nothing of the note to me or to Mother. One week later he raped me a second time. I forgot about the note until many years later, though I never saw it again.

Father's abuse occurred six more times with monthly regularity. Each time the scenario was relatively similar. I was always surprised by the suddenness of its start, and then the rapidity with which it ended. When it did, I breathed deeply. I strained to fill my lungs when the door closed and Father left, as if the air around me might soon evaporate. I sat still for a long period, clothed and dried, and opened my mouth wide, forcing great gulps of air down my throat, just like Mikey. I became light-headed from the saturation of oxygen in my blood, and I blacked-out for brief moments on occasion. When I left the room I walked with my fingers extended. I rubbed them across the silken texture of our couch, over woodwork and plaster walls. I grasped the smooth, cool surface of painted moldings. I wandered through the dark rooms and hallways of our home. I looked for doors that might lead me to a hidden passage, some secret place within our walls or below the basement. The house was perfectly quiet at those times, like our church on a weekday afternoon.

I never heard Father in his room or in other parts of the house after any of the rapes. He left me alone, to await my mother's return, to find my way back to the order of things. Often I wouldn't see him for a full day. He'd work late, and call just prior to dinner to tell Mother he'd run into some problem with materials and was obliged to finish. When I saw him a day or two later he'd take a fake punch at my chin or pinch my cheek. His fingers seemed very hard when he touched me, as if they'd shatter were he to strike an equally hard surface.

*

Father and I attended ten o'clock mass together every Sunday. After mass we walked the six blocks to our home, hand firmly in hand. We didn't speak until we got within sight of our house. At that time he asked me to tell him what the Priest's sermon was about. Father listened closely as I gave the best account I could of the lesson. He never questioned me about the meaning, but rather seemed to be interested in as close a recitation as I could give of the talk. One Sunday, the Gospel described Christ's miracle with loaves and fishes. The priest said this parable showed us the abundance of God's love, a love that was never ending. My father said to me – and I remember this clearly because of the rarity of his comments – "that's just like the love a father has for his son." He held my hand tight, all the way to our front steps where he let go.

The next night, as I showered, Father entered the bathroom, whistling. I noticed he lingered, sitting on the toilet bowl. When I was through washing, Father wrapped his arms tightly across my chest and held me until he'd finished. I remained motionless. I don't recall if there was physical pain. But in the intervening weeks between one event and the next, I walked around our house as if our entire family would soon vanish. I stared intently at the living room couch and mentally transcribed the orange, swirling pattern. I expected like them, it would soon be gone.

*

We drove on New Year's Eve to celebrate at my grandmother's house. Our family arrived at the dark housing project in New Brunswick and parked on the street in front of a high school that was built in the style of a southern mansion. In the apartment, my two uncles and two aunts were gathered around the kitchen table with their spouses. The conversation was loud, the table filled with dishes of potatoes and vegetables, turkey and stuffing. Tall bottles of soda and short bottles of beer sat at the table's end. The adults' voices rang through the apartment. They laughed even louder at the jokes Uncle Frank told. Each adult shouted over the other to be heard.

At midnight we watched grandmother's TV and counted down as the ball dropped on Times Square. The adults returned to the kitchen for champagne toasts. The youngest grandchildren were already close to sleep. My cousin Karen and I, the two eldest, mostly fought whenever we found ourselves alone. This particular year we sat quietly in the living room, and colored in a big blank book. At one point, Karen stood up across the room so no one could see her down the long hallway from the kitchen. Only I could watch her lift her dress, revealing white underwear and tights. She did it again, and yet again with a great smile. Her arms flew up as she held the dress's hem. She pulled it high over her head, laughing, giggling and dancing. I stood and situated myself in the corner behind an end table. A lamp burned brightly. I unzipped my fly and unhooked my pants. I pulled them down, down to my ankles, showing Karen my long underwear. We laughed joyously, whooping with loud voices, and reached near hysterical movement. Neither of us could stop, propelled on by each other's actions. Tears rolled from my eyes, and I could barely catch my breath. We grew more raucous with the passing minutes, and it seemed to me that we played like this for hours.

Without our notice, Father entered. I looked up. He loomed over me and grabbed my shirt collar, took three sharp cracks at my backside. I squirmed past the first, but the last two caught me square. If he hadn't been clutching my shirt I would have flown across the room. As it was, his forceful blows caused my legs to buckle.

"You never, ever, do that again." Father's teeth clenched. "I won't have it. Understand?"

I looked up at him through tearing eyes when he pulled my head back. I nodded. He curled his lip at Karen as he left the room.

A few days later was the last encounter I had with Father. My mother and brother were at a communion breakfast that had been planned for months. The living room curtains were open, bright winter sunlight streamed in from the street in the early morning. There were no doors to close us in. A show called "Wonderama" played on television. It was a show I watched every Sunday, and I looked forward to it for all the years of my childhood.

After Father finished with me, he left the room. The warmth of the sun and the television's glow lulled me into a near sleep state. There was a calm in that room that I've never felt since. I washed and dressed, and returned to the living room. The television was still on, but Father was gone.

*

The rapes never occurred again. Father continued to work in Asbury Park, his business prospered and expanded for a while until the riots of the late sixties turned everything sour. After that he complained about the poor and lazy people that began to enter our community. He worked as much and as often as he could, but jobs became more scarce as people moved away, or even abandoned their homes. He worked on our own house continually, filling in the long stretches between paying jobs. Ours stood out among the ill-kept, hollow homes in the neighborhood. It was beautifully painted with complementary pastel colors. Shutters bordered the windows and a sloped slate roof laid over ornate woodworked eaves. My father was outside as soon as there was enough light, until dusk made it hard to see. In bad weather he worked indoors. He built shelves and installed wainscoting, laid new hardwood floors and put in fine oak cabinets for the kitchen. When he finished in the evening, he sat at the table and ate without conversation, though he always asked my brother and I how school had been that day. We'd answer "fine," knew nothing more was desired. After dinner he left us for his living room chair and read a page or two of the newspaper before he fell asleep. Mother woke him only after we'd gone to bed. I heard his sleep-clumsy steps in the darkness as he made his way to their bedroom.

*

In high school I became part of the theater group. I acted in several productions in my junior and senior year. The lead role of Chino in West Side Story was given to me even though I was fair skinned and light-haired. My parents and Mikey came to see the show. I spotted them in the audience, whispering with the parents of one of my classmates. I lost my concentration for a beat when I noticed them, and only the off stage cue from the prompter saved me. After the performance, my parents met me at the back door of the auditorium. My father put his arm around me and pressed his face close to mine. His breath was warm on my neck and his slight stubble scratched me and sent a quick, cool shiver down my back. It felt like a shaft of silver had been injected into my spine. He had hardly touched me since I was eight.

"You are a very good son," he whispered.

*

When he was seventeen Mikey worked at the ShopRite supermarket. I arrived home from college three days before Thanksgiving. The phone rang the first night I was there. My father answered. His face was without expression and his body didn't move as he listened.

"Mikey was packing out fifty pound bags of onions and garlic. He had another attack. His heart stopped."

My father insisted on a closed coffin for Michael. During the wake Father spoke to no one but his youngest brother, who'd come back to New Jersey from San Diego for the first time in ten years. Mother and I sat beside each other. She wept while I greeted the few family members and friends who came.

We called for Chinese food for our Thanksgiving dinner. A very old man rode a small boy's bike up the walk to our house. He wore a white tee shirt and rain poncho. The brown bag he carried was stained with grease.

"Fifteen dollars." He handed me the bag and grease dripped onto my hand and pants.

"Thank you." I gave the man the money. He looked at me in silence for what seemed like a long time before he left without another word.

The next morning I packed my luggage.

"I'm leaving." It was three days before I'd planned to return to school. Mother cried and gave me a light kiss on my cheek. Father sat in his chair. After I passed my and Mikey's old bedroom, I thought of how he came to me during my childhood, how he removed his clothes and wrapped his hands around my stomach. I could hear once more his heavy drawn breath over the top of my head, feel the strain of his arms, the rocking of his pelvis, and the jabs at me like a mute poker.

I never saw him alive again.

*

I live in Houston now and work as an independent contractor for new technologies corporations. So many years after Mikey's death, and now Father's, I wake in the middle of each night. I see my brother and my parents, and think of my childhood, which appears like a film faded from age, the colors muted, blotched and discolored. I rise in the dry heat and make my way to the kitchen for a beer. I sit naked in an old wooden rocker. The can sweats its cold onto my leg and stomach, moisture drips. I stare out the window of my high-rise to the skyline of the large, sleeping city. It rolls before me, pins of light puncturing the blackness. I begin each night, trying to remember the precise details of my life.

August
Holli Flanagan

In an August heat, I tell my mother I'm still married. I promise that the only difference is the boy I vowed my life to is ready to be herself. Days later, in our worst moment, my mother says she doesn't have to be happy for me to love me, reaches gently into my chest, and pulls my lungs out. She follows me around most days now, dragging the pinkness of me in her acrylic-nailed grip. At the grocery store, I wrestle the shrill ghost of Elizabeth Taylor perfume in the frozen pizza aisle. I rattle her, violently whisper that she belongs 400 miles away in a cluttered bathroom, looming over the nail polish stain a nine-year-old left in her rush to be pretty. When the insomnia comes, phantom melodies of *He's got the whole world in His hands* claw at my eardrums and remind me how easily I used to sink into sleep. I avoid mirrors first thing in the morning, eyes shut tight before I finally have to stare back at her eyes, her hair, the curve of her nose. I do my makeup, trying not to look. She critiques my lipstick, my too-thick eyebrows, the ragged hole in my chest and what spills from it. I have leaked again, watery stench running all over the floor. I can't stay closed or clean enough.

Stepfamily
Daniel Schall

we knew that well-   water beard   before the face   all-encompassing beard

swaddling you   in wooly amnesia   beard before nose   beard consumed eyes
lips

  brown cloud   bursting up there   near the ceiling   that would rain confetti

when he sniffed her out   our mama   probing her   like a cone of honeysuckle

mornings before school   in the kitchen   coffee and goat blood   followed

by seared eggs   aromas closed   by hot irons into nostrils   his mouth groped

nothing   would know itself inside there   he never smiled   not once   the truly right

  and just   he said   don't need to   time came to leave   to molt into new people

mama flew   up to her chest   of drawers   matted herself down   demanded evidence

that we existed   he pressed   the truck driver into snapping   a polaroid   here

we stood   washed out at strange angles   the trailer   bleached canvas behind us

clasped in his arms   my sister   child slung   in the cradle of a wave   and her
frowning

  turning   refusing the lens   untrained still   in the art of survival

Mom's Cheesecake Always Tasted Better
Katie Hébert

i hear her name echo in a restaurant and jolt like it is my own / everyone at the table serves me sad eyes as they catch me not finding her / another woman with blonde hair answers / *"what kind of cheesecake does your dad like?"* / i think about my mother's answers /

i hear her name in the dining hall / someone crying out for *anna* / me too / and she does not answer / she will not ever answer / but this anna does / they find each other / hug and laugh / and i long for that again / they eat omelets / like mom used to make /

i drive by a neighborhood i shouldn't know this much about / the corner taco bell / the rochard bar across the street / earl's bar / mount sinai's bridge / looking over train tracks / the moon is shining / the uber driver does not notice / i do not notice / at first / i watch the rain fall into ashes /

she yells at me over the phone / but this is not her voice / and this is not to me / still blood though / still red wine / still a red car / still red bricks on a house washing away / still hearing a ghost of her in everyone / driving through tunnels and turnpikes and timelines / sounds of a broken lineage /

they ask me about dessert again / mom's cheesecake always tasted better /
"does he like key lime?" / reminiscent of a sour goodbye /
"tiramisu?" / nothing can wake her now /
"just pick one" / how would you like mourning to taste /
"there are so many flavors" / you will only have one mother

Perfecting a Future Tense
Keli Osborn

My brother likes to send messages about the past.
Tomorrow, he could pay tribute to an aging rocker
who's just died, and we'll trade lyrics from songs

we heard decades ago, crammed into the back seat
of our family Corvair. When the ghost of Capote
shows up in the news, my brother will remind me

about the time we half-watched "In Cold Blood,"
fingers over our eyes as our parents bowled next door.
If there were an anniversary card for natural disasters,

he'd send one for the Mount St. Helens eruption,
prod me to recall the ash coating windshields, grit
on our teeth hundreds of miles to the south.

The past is a big country. My brother and I lived there
together. If quantum physics means what I think,
we might be living there yet. I'd like to send him

a message from the future, but what could I say?
That we are each of us bound, however fleeting—
wherever home. I hope my brother gets the message.

On the night I had hot dogs and baked beans for dinner
Susan Kolon

it was your birthday, little sister.
You got a new bike, sheened

in lustful boysenberry, tassels
hanging from sky-high handlebars

and I was jealous. You let me
boss you when we played, change

the channel, best you always.
That night I staged a race, hurried

you through supper, hot dogs
and baked beans —I ate two,

had to outdo you. Riding
in the breeze, your blonde

locks waving, my pixie stuck
to my forehead in the humidity.

You were ahead and I turned
my front wheel into your rear.

You fell, of course,
like I wanted you to.

The baby blue Volkswagen couldn't
stop, burning rubber, skid marks

on the pavement. A leg of plaster
and five stitches on your tender

face. For that hot July summer,
your pedaling days were done.

And you knew it was me
but you never told.

after her treatment fails, mama packs a suitcase of generous proportions

 Mary Alice Dixon

first went
her memory
tucked in a red clay teacup
wrapped in silver scarves
then she added two lilies
only she could see

mama left behind
pink ribbons
and half-moon scars
where once
she wore her breasts
but proudly
took her wrinkles
and claws of feral lust

when she had gone beyond
the reach of customs
mama called
keep this while I'm away

then in my hands
she placed
her memory
wrapped in silver scarves
and lilies
only i could see

Trans-Allegheny
Timothy Dodd

Mother could have been here.
I could've been here. In a bed.
In a little room. Down Main
Street in Weston, across West

Fork River. In the mammoth
sandstone building. Underneath
a white and green tower, steeple.
Mental illness is our majority

and we are looking for paradise:
try lobotomy, malarial, insulin
shock, electroconvulsive, deep
sleep, hydro, cardiazol therapy.

Strap and sedate are now seat
belts, caffeine: drive in, park,
eat at a little bistro and walk
over the bridge. Pay by Cash

App for a tiny tour. Stare inside
with strangers at all the silence,
vacant rooms, empty air: numb
knowing we've all floated away.

Father Figures
Amy-Lenna Bryce

Grandad carried the spectre of his father
on his back like other people carry their children.
When he leant forward in his armchair to pick up his beer,

you could see the shadow clinging
around his neck with the strength of dockyard cranes.
He never talked about the man on his back,

preferring to submerge himself in bitter brown drink,
until his coal-smudged childhood ran off the slipways of his mind.
Welded in his ways, Grandad wore his many fights

on the bridge of his crooked nose. Forged on fear
and quenched in his mistakes, he was brittle,
a man straining under the weight of his own history,

too stiff to bend himself into the shape of an apology.
When Grandad died, my father drove and collected me
from outside the port-a-cabin ward that housed the corpse,

one car door and a temporary wall separating father and son,
closer together than they had been for years.
My father cried, not for any loss he felt but instead relief

and as the car hurtled home, the radio incongruous between us,
I became aware of how my father sagged over the steering wheel.
I watched him shrink into a little boy, crushed

under the ghost of his father. The car door closed
and for a second I glimpsed a new, heavy shadow hanging
around my father's neck, like a blackout curtain in a bedroom window.

Another son, with another father, anchoring
him to a childhood he would rather forget.
How far down the branch does the damage go?

I wonder, if I dug up the roots of my family tree,
would I find an unbroken line of cruelty and unfulfilled dreams?
Each son's birthright: his father's trauma in the lash of a belt.

Haunting Me
Roger Funston

My father summoned me to his apartment after years of estrangement. Shocked when I saw him, not knowing he had been ill for some time. He was only 65. Had a most distinctive smell. I later realized this was the smell of pending death. The memory haunting me for some time.

He showed me his important papers, his Will designating me as Executor and Trustee. Asked me to be caregiver for my disabled mother, her wish, something he had chosen not to do. Instead, walking out on her and moving into a furnished apartment. Separated but not divorced, I later learned he told women in his building he was single.

He had had a quadruple bypass. His kidneys had failed. Not a candidate for a kidney transplant due to poor health. The daily dialysis straining his already weak heart. He knew he was dying and didn't want to die alone. So he planned to move back in with my mother.

My younger brother was very close to my father. He had come over to help him pack. Found him dead on the floor, dialysis bag in his hand. My brother called me in a panic.

Sitting next to my father's body, waiting for the deputy sheriff and coroner.
A cool, rainy December day. Black clouds, dark sky, dark room. Remembering. We did few father/son things together. My parents going off on vacation, leaving the kids behind. Few family outings, often filled with drama. He hurt his fingers once when it was struck by a model airplane propeller, running back into the house. But he didn't cry. I never saw him cry.

Lots of anger, raging about relatives. None of them were any good, except his parents. Even the ones I liked. Screaming matches with my adolescent sister through a closed and locked bathroom door. Too much smoking, drinking, unhealthy food.

Constant put downs in my childhood for being a sensitive Louie. I wasn't good at sports. He once chased me down and wrestled me to the floor as we both grunted. Too many moments of ridicule and criticism. I later jokingly called it the Peter Funston school of self-esteem; building yourself up by tearing the other guy down. At the time, I didn't understand that this was emotional abuse leading to low self-effacement, sensitivity to criticism and needing to prove my worth. It took me most of my twenties to get my groove back.

He had forsaken law school to go into business. His business failed so he became a traveling salesmen. Lots of regrets, fighting his demons. He tried to push me to become a lawyer, to take the path he didn't follow. But I was committed to environmental science. He never understood my passion for the outdoors and nature. I could hardly wait to leave home at 18.

Waiting for the funeral parlor men. They arrived wearing black trench coats. Strapped him to a gurney. Lifted it vertically to fit into the elevator to take him downstairs. Treated like unclaimed freight.

A most depressing funeral. The one friend he hadn't alienated was there, along with relatives who felt obligated to attend. Not a celebration of a life well lived. Made me think about who I was touching in my life and how many people would attend my funeral.

I only visited by father's grave once, soon after the funeral. Perhaps he couldn't help who he was. Or maybe he could have but he was just an asshole. As an adult, I could think of so many ways I could have pushed back, but I wasn't able to do so as a child. I rarely think of these times now, putting them in a box on a shelf. But the way he lived his life has guided me on my path to living mine.

Driving You Home
Shelly Reed Thieman

At rest after eighty-one years,
you make me laugh once more
the evening of cremation
with your false eyelashes, mystic
heather eye shadow, dollar store
sprigs of lilacs and bluebells
in your left hand, a bingo card
and dauber in the other.

The sun spreads apricot
over the western horizon.
In the parking lot I watch smoke
rise from the flue, swirl
like the skirt of your square
dance dress, disappear
toward the hemline of dusk.
While stars come back to life,
the moon mimics your pin-fire
opal dangling on its delicate
chain at my breastbone.

Inside, a stranger sweeps
your holy dust from the chamber,
cremains warm as the lap I loved.
I carry you home in the brass
pearl-footed box you bought
last time we went thrifting.
We drive slowly as your black
checkers always did, moving
across our gameboard.

Reminiscing on One Rural Summer
Shelly Reed Thieman

Not by choice, Sister and I spent a week in summer at our grandmother's house in a tiny, rural Iowa town. There wasn't a damn thing to do or see but walk the miniature cemetery or stare at the peeling water tower. Our shared bedroom was upstairs, thirteen of them. Every single one groaned with the slightest of weight placed. We were not allowed to come downstairs during the night. If we needed to pee or *God forbid* poop, we had to use a rickety commode. There was a dreadful cuckoo clock in grandmother and her husband's bedroom that blared every hour on the hour. It was a terrifying reminder we weren't in the luxury of our own home.

Her third husband would pat us on our butts when we passed, make a clicking sound with his mouthful of dentures. One morning during stale cereal he told us their dog had died during the night, that it had defecated its internal organs. We both cried.

That week was hotter than a billy goat with a blow torch. Getting dressed one morning, we both chose handmade halter tops and matching shorts. When our grandmother spotted us doing cartwheels in the yard, she came flying out of nowhere, yelling *Get in the damn house! You both look like whores!* That afternoon, we were ordered to walk to the mart to buy milk and bread. So we did. With the leftover change, Sister used the payphone to call Mom and beg her to come get us.

aghast
step grandfather's nightstand
vaseline and porn

One Less Open
S. Michael Wilson

Kinsey hated eating on the road.

Choosing where to eat was always the biggest hassle for him. Everything else is decided by corporate or necessity. There was no real choice when it came to the travel itself. He flew where he had to go, and the nearest airport was the obvious first choice. He could technically state an airline preference, but despite the occasional good experience on Delta or a bad one on US Air, all airlines were basically the same. And unless McGonagall suddenly promoted him to CEO or he became independently wealthy, he would always fly economy.

Technically, the only real choice Kinsey faced was dinners during the show itself. Breakfast was less of a choice than it was a coin-toss between the hotel's version of a continental breakfast[1] or an overpriced coffee and bagel/danish/pastry at the nearest coffee shop. Lunch was even less of an option, as the odds were always against him eating anything even closely resembling a meal during a day on the floor. The average workplace "lunch break" barely leaves enough time for the procurement and enjoyment of a meal when in the familiar territory of a corporate cafeteria or nearby strip-mall sub shop. Put that time constraint on grabbing a bite to eat in between computer training sessions with a small army of part-time retail employees in the middle of Utah, and he might as well choke down a stale granola bar in between training sessions and save those hunger pangs for the end of the day.

He had spied a shabby little diner within walking distance of the hotel during the previous night's shuttle ride, and that was where he wound up after the booth was wrapped and the show floor shut down for the night. It was an old-fashioned diner with a lunch bar at one end, and he perched himself on a padded stool at the end opposite the cash register. The stool was stiff and unyielding, and his back was practically screaming for some long-awaited lumbar support, but he didn't like taking up a booth or table by himself, so he did his best to get comfortable by slouching in a way that hopefully did not appear overly despondent.

There was a party of eight or nine taking up two tables in the dining area, which was separated from the booth and lunch counter section by a waist-high brick wall topped with fake ferns. There were other groups of diners scattered at the tables and booths throughout the building, but this larger gathering demanded attention. They were obviously some kind of extended family; you could tell by the way they were just a little bit louder than the other parties. Not necessarily rowdy or disruptive, but just a half a decibel above what Kinsey would consider an acceptable volume in a restaurant. Maybe it was just him. Nobody else around seemed to notice.

Kinsey wondered if he seemed to notice. Could people tell what he was thinking about them just by looking at his face? It was a passing fear, but not one he could devote any real concern to. He'd spent so many years masking his contempt and frustration with people both over the phone and in person that there could be little doubt about his ability to keep a poker face. If even a fraction of what he felt about the people he often trained while on the road was readily apparent in his expressions and attitude, he would have been fired a long time ago.

Kinsey ordered a tuna melt with fries, then counted the minutes of the most awkward part of eating out alone, the silent wait for the food to arrive. It's different in a bar. In a bar he could pretend to watch the game on the television, exchange pleasantries with fellow nearby loners, or even study the bottles lined up behind the bar as if he was a connoisseur of distilled spirits. But when he was sitting alone in a restaurant, it was a whole new level of social restrictions. There aren't any mounted TVs to gaze at, striking up a conversation with strangers feeding their kids or enjoying a Date Night is out of the question, and they don't even let leave the menu after taking the order, so pretending to reread the appetizers section isn't even an option. All he could do was sit there, act casual, and occasionally glance around the room while attempting to avoid direct eye contact with anybody so he merely appeared curious without being creepy. He had intentionally left the book back at the hotel to avoid having to read it while he relaxed after the show, an action he had obviously not thought through.

Kinsey hadn't even made his first casual glance around the room when a commotion started at the large family table.

"Excuse me?"

It was an older man at the table that raised his voice, and just those two words were enough to indicate that he was clearly agitated and confrontational. Kinsey didn't turn to look, but noticed others already twisting in their seats to locate the source.

"I just asked if you wanted cheese with your omelet." The waitress answered hesitantly. There was no attitude in her voice, a sure sign of weakness. She wasn't ready for a fight.

"Why would you ask me if I wanted cheese on my omelet?" The waitress hesitated, unsure of what response would calm the old man down. He took her silence as his cue to continue.

"I ordered a Western omelet," he said. There was an awkward pause. Kinsey did not glance over to see if the waitress nodded.

"Western omelets do not come with cheese."

"Right," the waitress agreed. "That's why I asked if you wanted cheese."

"Why would I order a Western omelet if I wanted an omelet with cheese on it?"

"Sir, I was just trying to..."

"A Western omelet doesn't come with pickles on it. Why don't you ask me if I want pickles on it?"

"Pop," a younger male voice interjected, "Why don't you just let her finish. It's okay, miss. Just put him down for the Western omelet, that'll be fine."

"I don't want the omelet now! She's already mentioned cheese, so she has cheese in her head. Somewhere between here and the kitchen all she's going to remember is cheese, and I'm going to end up with cheese on my god damn Western omelet."

"Pop, she's not going to put cheese on..."

"Why in the hell is everybody always trying to put cheese on my plate? I'll bet if I ordered French toast she'd ask me if I wanted cheese on it."

"Grampa" - a younger female voice this time, possibly a teenager - "you don't even like French toast."

"I don't like cheese either, but that doesn't seem to be stopping anyone from trying to smother my food with it. You know what, I'm screwed no matter what I order now, so why don't you just bring me an order of French toast covered in cheese."

"I can come back in a few minutes to take your order if you like." Kinsey could hear the waitress' voice backing away slowly.

Kinsey finally looked over in the direction of the table. He could see the man with the cheese issue clearly. He was definitely older, coarse grey hair trailing out the back of his baseball cap. He was as intimidating physically as he was verbally, broad-shouldered and barrel-chested. If you had to guess at his profession based on looks alone, truck driver or retired bouncer would be anybody's first two guesses. The waitress was behind him, but he was looking straight ahead as he talked to her.

"You try to sabotage my first order, and now you won't even take my new one? I already told you - I want French toast with cheese. If you come back to this table without a plate of French toast smothered in some kind of cheese, I'm throwing whatever you bring me across the room."

The rest of what Kinsey assumed were family members continued to try and calm Pop down while the waitress just stood there, undoubtedly afraid that walking away would incur an even greater wrath from the old man. There was no discernible logic to Pop's arguments; normal fight or flight instincts were untrustworthy. So the waitress froze and waited for either the other family members to subdue him or the man to flip the table over and come after her with a fork. Kinsey turned back on his stool and stared intently at the flat grey backsplash behind the coffee urns.

The commotion at the distant table triggered a childhood memory buried so deep in Kinsey's subconscious that remembering it almost felt like a hallucination, as if somebody had flipped a switch in his head and started an old home movie from somebody else's past.

It had been one of those family vacations that comedy routines and sitcom plots were born from. His father had fallen into the trap that most middle-aged family men become snagged in after countless years of soul-rendering labor to maintain a lower-middle class existence of constant struggling and diminishing returns. He had become obsessed with the idea of the "Family Vacation" to such a point that it became more stressful than foregoing the vacation all together and staying at work. There was so much significance and necessity tied up in the expectation of a flawless family getaway, by the time it actually happened the entire journey was wracked with mounting tension and dread. The insistence that nothing could go wrong with the trip did little more than increase everyone's awareness of the inevitability of something going wrong. It was like waiting for a firecracker to explode in your hand.

They had stopped at a highway service station an hour into West Virginia for bathroom breaks and snack replenishments, miles still to go before reaching a prepaid motel that seemed further away the longer they spent on the road. Dad was already on edge by the time they returned to the car because he had been forced to track down Kinsey and Mom when both of them failed to show up at the fifteen-minute rendezvous spot between the broken water fountains and the half-empty pamphlet rack.

He found Kinsey first, five minutes beyond the scheduled meeting time. Kinsey had been playing with the hot air hand driers in the bathroom, spinning the elbow-shaped blowers upward and thrusting his face into the screaming jet of heat. One minute he was squinting into the black tunnel of the hand dryer, his hair leaping up from his forehead as he tried his hardest to breath back into the blower, mimicking the noise with a deep "Ororrorororororororo" in between giggles,[3] the next minute he was being dragged by his wrist behind an angry Dad in search of his other deserter.

Mom was discovered next to the big hand-crank machine that charges you four quarters to flatten a penny with an impression memorializing your trip to the service area. She had already pressed the images of an eagle, an American flag, and the shape of West Virginia with the name of the state across it on three now uselessly thin and ovoid pennies, and was in the process of disfiguring a fourth coin with the image of a Black Bear[4] playing with its cub when Dad approached her from the opposite side of the machine. No words were exchanged, but Dad's impatient glare was met and held by Mom's steady, defiant stare as she slowly - ever so slowly - finished the last two rotations of the big crank handle, not even blinking until the imagined silence of the bustling souvenir shop was broken by the tiny plink of the flattened Black Bear penny dropping into the return tray.

Not a word was spoken as they made their way across the parking lot and into the second-hand Renault Encore. They had been gone long enough for the late afternoon sun to bake away the last of the residual air conditioning they had left trapped in the car, which Dad somehow indicated was the fault of Kinsey and Mom with a prolonged stiffening of his shoulders. They all shut their doors and settled in as Dad started the car and cranked the AC to battle the newly heat-infested interior. As everybody adjusted themselves and basked in the refreshing arctic air blasting from the dashboard, Mom opened and closed the passenger side door again with a sharp thud.

Dad froze.

"What was that?" He asked the question without turning his head away from the steering wheel, which from the back seat was quite unsettling to young Kinsey.

"Hmmm?"

"What was that?"

"What was what?"

"With the door."

"I don't know what you're talking about."

"The door. You opened and shut it again."

"I wasn't sure if I closed it properly."

"You weren't sure."

"No."

"You couldn't remember if you had shut the door?"

"That's not what I said. I *said* that I wasn't sure if the door had closed properly."

"Because suddenly you're inexperienced at opening and closing car doors." Dad was still looking straight ahead, even though Mom's head was pointed right at him.

"Why," Mom asked, "are you making such a big deal over me shutting the door again."

"Because now your door has one less open."

"One less open?"

"Yes. One less open."

"So there's a cut-off for how many times I can open the door."

"Every car door has a finite number of opens, and you've just wasted one of yours."

"That doesn't make any sense. Car doors do not have a limited number of opens."

"It makes perfect sense." Dad finally turned and faced Mom. "We do not live in a magical world of make believe. Things do not last forever. There is friction and entropy and degradation and decay, and everything that exists only has a certain amount of physical interactions it can take until it ceases to function properly. These are universal laws of physics at play here. Every door has a limited number of times that it can be opened and closed before it no longer functions properly, and now your door has one less open than my door because you couldn't remember the sound a properly closed car door makes."

"I know exactly what sound a closed car door makes. It sounds like this." Mom opened and closed the door again, shutting it with more force this time so the THUD was louder.

"Cute. Keep using up that door's opens, and you know what's going to happen if the car suddenly skids off the road and rolls into a pond? I'll be able to get out of the car and swim to safety because my door has plenty of opens left. Your door, on the other hand, will be all out of opens, and you'll spend the last few moments of your life before you drown to death struggling with your door handle. Do you have any idea how selfish that is?"

"How *what*? Selfish?"

"That's right, selfish. Here you are, flapping your door open and shut like you're trying to fan the pavement, using up all of its opens and making me a widower[5] in the process. You think it's fair that your son has to grow up without his mother because she couldn't figure out how car doors work?"

"Don't you drag your son into your little world of madness. Nobody is going to die because I closed the car door a few more times than you did."

"Remember that when you're at the bottom of a lake trying to breathe water because you'd rather turn your half of the car into a deathtrap rather than admit I'm right."

"I'll be sure to do that. I'll even write it on the inside of the windshield in lipstick before my lungs finally give out. 'He Was Right, One Less Open.' Maybe you can even put it on my tombstone as a warning to others."

"You'd like that, wouldn't you?"

"Yes, I'd love to drown at an early age in a late-model foreign import and then be openly mocked on my tombstone. As a matter of fact, I'm pretty sure I listed that under Future Ambitions in my high school yearbook."

"I don't doubt it for a minute. But no, I can't do it. I can't let you destroy this family out of spite."

Dad shifted in his seat and, after a dramatic pause, opened and closed his door twice, slamming it shut each time hard enough to make the window rattle.

"There. Now we both have the same number of opens."

"Oh my God." Mom gasped in mock horror. "What have you done? Now you'll drown with me. There will be nobody to survive and spread my cautionary tale."

"It had to be done. I've already made enough sacrifices just so I could grow old and gray with you, I'll be damned if I'm going to spend my retirement alone. I'd rather condemn myself to a watery grave then give you the satisfaction."

This was followed by a silent moment of glaring and wordless accusations before Mom spoke next.

"You know what? If this is going to be the kind of attitude I can look forward to in my golden years, I don't think I want to survive our next underwater car accident." With that, she opened and closed her car door again, which he responded to by doing the same.

The next few minutes seemed to go on forever to young Kinsey, who silently witnessed the escalation of the argument into a cacophony of slamming doors. The repeated concussions in the enclosed space caused by the doors opening and slamming shut became increasingly deafening in the depths of the back seat, and both parents added to the noise, punctuating the slams with angry shouts of "One less open!" The car rocked side to side with the momentum of the slamming doors as Mom and Dad found a sort of rhythmic unity in their battle of diminishing opens.

It all finally came to a head when Dad leaned over Mom's lap to open and shut her door and yelled "Fine! You die first! See if I care!" She made a move to lean over Dad's lap to do the same, but he shifted to block her from his door, and she finally ceded the argument with a shrug of her shoulders, a fluttering of hands, and a mumbled "Whatever. Let's just go."

The interior of the car was still warm and muggy, and the first fifteen minutes of the final two hour drive to the hotel was physically and mentally stifling. No words were spoken the entire way to the hotel, and both tempers and temperatures cooled considerably by the time they pulled into the parking lot of the Eazy-Zway Motor Lodge.

Things almost took a turn for the worse again when Mom and Dad found young Kinsey unwilling to get out of the car.

At first they thought he was upset about watching them argue, but the truth the eventually came to light was that Kinsey had spent the entire ride to the hotel obsessing over which of the rear car doors had been opened more. Not only was he now completely unsure of which door to try first if Dad drove the car into a lake - which now seemed like an inevitability - but he couldn't decide which door was the safest one to open without taking away too many of its opens. He was frozen with the fear that either choice would lead to his future drowning, and so he just sat in the center of the rear bench seat with the full intention of taking his meals back there for the rest of his life, or at least until Dad drove the car into a duck pond and killed them all.

Mom was quicker to pick up on the problem - as most Moms are - and she diffused the situation by convincing Kinsey to roll down the window and climb out of the car that way. They could have just as easily opened the door for him from the outside, of course, but by that point even Mom and Dad were a little spooked by the whole ordeal. They let him sleep in the same bed as them that night, and everybody was in good cheer when they left the hotel the following morning in search of fast food breakfast meals in Styrofoam travel trays. The incident was not mentioned for the remainder of the trip, and nobody opened a car door unless it was absolutely necessary.

The relevance of this memory emerging at this particular moment in time eluded Kinsey. He did not consider the door incident to be representative of his childhood. It was an aberration, not a typical example of their family dynamic. Perhaps that was why it had been so readily forgotten. In fact, he was pretty sure that he wasn't the only one who had forced that moment out of mind. The more he thought about it, he was pretty sure the phrase 'One Less Open' was never spoken aloud afterward, even in jest. It was as if they had all come to a silent agreement that it was never to be mentioned ever again. A dirty family secret, buried out in the backyard amongst the zinnias.

Dad's behavior in that memory, isolated from everything else, was not a flattering portrayal. He had been downright scary at that particular moment, yet Kinsey could not remember ever fearing his father. Even in this memory, it was the looming specter of malfunctioning car doors and unscheduled lake-bottom detours that had frightened him, not his father's over-the-top antics. His childhood had been a fairly happy one, all things considered. Sure, there were the occasional bad times and family arguments, but nothing even bordering on the physical or emotional abuse that other people liked to complain or brag about. He never flinched involuntarily if Dad suddenly raised an arm, or avoided making eye contact with him in his recliner when walking through the living room. He loved Dad then, still did. If any permanent harm had been rendered by Kinsey's parents during his developmental years, there was not a doubt in his mind that the damage was unintentional.

Not that they were ideal parents. Kinsey was convinced Mom and Dad had never been fully prepared for parenthood. He didn't resent them for it. If anything, it was the noble character flaw that fully humanized them in his eyes, the realization that throughout his childhood they had been just as confused and lost as him. Punishments or reprimands that seemed stupid then were just as ludicrous to him now in hindsight, like Dad grounding him after spending entire weekends trying unsuccessfully to teach him the proper way to mow the lawn,[6] or Mom's assurances that the bullies at school were just jealous of Kinsey's superior math skills.[7] They were just as clueless as he was.

As far as Kinsey was concerned, very few adults if any were actually prepared for parenthood. Whenever he was around people with children, he would marvel at the authority with which they made the most preposterous statements he had ever heard. There was never any hesitancy or doubt; they just knew. Either that, or their parents had lived by the same principles or ideals regarding child rearing, which have must have been the right ones, because look how good they turned out.

It was the ruler argument all over again. Where do people learn to be parents? From their own parents. Whether they emulate them with pride or swear that they will never - EVER - treat their child the same way they were treated, their parents are still the major influence behind parenting philosophies. And where did their parents learn their parenting skills? From their parents, of course, and the chain of mistakes and regrets extends back beyond the nuclear family into the dawn of civilization, with each generation of parents making it up as they go and passing trial and error off as the wisdom of the ages. Where is the room for growth when each generation ends up reinventing the wheel?

"I dare you to tell me to calm down again. Just one more time. Tell me to calm down, and let's see what happens together."

It was the old man's voice that brought Kinsey out of this thoughts, followed almost immediately by a loud crash. Kinsey joined the rest of the diner patrons in looking over at the family gathering, and saw that the old man was now standing. The waitress had been joined by a tall, slender man with a mustache and a tie - most likely the manager - and they were both stepping back from the table as the old man hoisting the heavy wooden chair he had been sitting on over his head. Kinsey could think of no good reason for him to be lifting a chair over his head, and the expressions of the other onlookers told him that he was not alone. Besides the one that kept calling the old man pop, the rest of the family was still seated at the table, as if waiting on deck for the storm to pass.

Kinsey wasn't hungry anymore. The padded cushion in the center of the lunch counter stool had deflated enough under his weight that the metal rim of the seat was now noticeably pressing into his ass and upper thighs. He tried to signal a waiter to cancel his order, but the restaurant staff was a little preoccupied with the elderly gentleman now chasing the manager around the fern wall with the chair still raised in the air.

Kinsey felt guilty about it, but decided it was best to slip out without canceling his order before things escalated. That guilt diminished slightly when the sound of breaking glass came from behind just before he crossed the highway. He didn't look back.

1. Originally, a 'Continental' Breakfast referred to the cold, less formal morning meal an Englishman might expect - cold cereal and pastries in lieu of more substantial fare like kippers and eggs - while traversing the European mainland, or "Continent," during the glory days of Britain's globalization pyramid scheme. Since this type of breakfast is no longer geared specifically towards English travelers, and Europe ceased being referred to as "the continent" shortly after the sun resumed setting on the British Empire, hotels now use the label of 'Continental' to replace less marketable yet more accurate descriptions of the breakfast option they now offer their patrons, such as "Sad" or "Disappointing." ↑

2. Kinsey was increasingly convinced that his wife had begun planning her social gatherings around his business travels so he would be unable to attend. He had not, however, confronted her with his suspicions for fear that she would stop doing so. ↑

3. While the events that transpired shortly after would be forgotten for decades, this particular moment would remain at the forefront of Kinsey's mind as one of the happiest moments of his childhood. ↑

4. The Black Bear was declared the state animal of West Virginia in 1954 based on a poll conducted by a Division of Natural Resources, condemning future residents of West Virginia to a state animal based not on geographical or ecological importance, but instead on the lack of creativity demonstrated by the majority of the state. ↑

5. One of those words that has never made sense to Kinsey. If a 'Widow' is a woman whose husband has died, then adding suffix 'er' - which typically designates a person's occupation, characteristic, or action - should reasonably mean that a 'Widower' is somebody who causes someone to become a widow, and not merely the male equivalent of a widow. Having only a partial grasp of the contradictions and inconsistencies of the grammatical laws ruling the English language at the time, young Kinsey was somewhat confused as to why his mother's death by drowning would motivate his father to run around killing other people's wives. ↑

6. Much of the problem had been Dad's insistence in dividing the front and back lawns into quadrants that had to be mowed in perfectly perpendicular lines. Young Kinsey's repeated inability to keep the push-mower on a straight path irritated Dad to the point that he strapped a compass to the mower push bar and marked across the lawn with clothesline and tent stakes. Young Kinsey's grounding occurred shortly after he tried to follow the needle on the compass and ran over one of the metal tent stakes with the mower. ↑

7. A proud young Kinsey once showed Mom a fourth grade fractions quiz with a perfect score. From that moment on, Mom would tell anyone who cared to listen how her child prodigy would one day walk the halls of NASA reciting formulas and brushing chalk off his expensive tweed jackets. Kinsey never showed her any test scores after that. ↑

Tuck In
John Grey

I imagine him
reeling up the creaky stairs.

I hear his voice
mutter something
which translates as
"I have come
to put the kibosh
on your happiness."

No slap of his hand
as he enters the room,
no falling down drunk,
though the stench of his breath
could break backboards.

Just more noise,
turns on his heels,
and departs.

It was his version
of tucking me in
on a Friday night.

Blankets, smell,
fear and relief –
I still can't get comfortable.

Then and Now
Diane Funston

If I had never left Rochester thirty years ago
I never would have known San Diego,
raised my children far from family ghosts.

If I had bought that old Victorian house
I would have cluttered it up with the past,
instead of the glorious skylit present

If my ex-husband had never abandoned me
I never would've known a good solid man
who took all of us on without hesitation.

If I had been a stay at home mom
maybe I wouldn't have cherished my boys as much,
each moment a gift not a chore.

If we would have stayed in our Tehachapi cabin
I never would've known true loneliness
of the gray landscape of central Nevada.

If I could've kept my Great Dane
I wouldn't have known the entire spectrum
of how cruel a husband my ex was.

If I had moved back to Rochester after the divorce
I never would have met my now-husband's
crooked smile and generous true love.

If I had not taken another chance at trust
I'd have never traveled Europe, Australia, or the tropics
without the heavy baggage of my past.

If I had hugged a huge soft polar bear
I never would have still been alive
to enjoy the real world apart from the fantasy.

My Fingers Were Not Swollen
Ana Martinez

My father's triggering smile was ready to pounce,
when he announced he had not eaten in three days.
On our video call he bragged about the ease of his morning hike,
despite the lack of solid nourishment for over 72 hours. I winced
when he lifted his shirt and pinched

the tiniest of midsections
on a popsicle stick frame.
Declaring the progress while noting the work yet to be done.
I focused down on my ring, the silver corset
that had been feeling quite snug.

Later I failed
to fight the urge to download the calorie counting app.
The dusty scale played peekaboo from behind the trash can.
When the pounds began to zipline down
the narrative should be that I would mirror him in pride.
Instead I choked on familiar resentment.

Because I'd been here before.
Nauseous by all the times I've betrayed my own values,
double dog dared myself never to touch another sweet in my life,
sweetness only earned if I could make myself sick
enough to call the therapist again.

My eyes blurred with disappointment and fell on my hands
as I mourned an alternate version of myself:

My father singing praises at my fingers dancing
on piano keys, making workplace desk altars
to my tiny play doh roses and dexterous origami swans.
Him cheering my strength at the monkey bars,
taking me to learn how to hold a tennis racquet for the first time.

His tender changing of my bandaids after I lost a nail,
wailed so hard when I jammed a door on my hand.
He reassured me how well it would heal,

that recovery was meant for accidental harm,
not self-inflicted disorders as I learned later on.

A version of me that isn't stuck on a memory of a sneered
"Are your fingers swollen, or are you just fat?"

Wanda's Boy
Peter Conrad

"I picked these up from the shore of the Beaufort Sea," Mary, an Inuit elder said. "You keep the one that has your initial in it." Paul saw the larger stone had two colours: light grey marking a P in dark grey. The second piece was light grey. "You give the other one to your mother when you find her, then you will always be together." She held her hand out to Paul. He reacted putting out his accepting palm. She dropped to stones into his hand. They were in Paul's tiny office with tinted blue walls at the Heritage Foundation in Edmonton, Alberta where he was a historian-writer, his Master of Arts degree in history paid off.

Paul's heart pounded, he had told no one he was adopted. His family had always denied it when others asked, "Where did you come from?" He looked different: athletic, did well in school and got along others.

"We recognize others like ourselves," Mary said. "You know that I was adopted by a very important man." Mary was holding her red parka with drummers across the bottom, just above the fur lining. This was the day she would return to the north.
She had been adopted by one of the most successful journalists in Canada, producing renown books about the country's history.

"Thank you," said Paul.

"You will look for her, but you already know who she is in your heart," said Mary.
Paul nodded.

Paul's birth certificate said he was born in Hinton to Edna and her husband Greg. From Paul's earliest memories, everyone who first met his brothers and sisters would ask, "Where did you come from?" Paul wandered *who are these people* and *why am I with them*?

Before Paul arrived, the family had always lived in the trailer park in Hinton. There was a photo that Paul saw many times of his grandfather and his two uncles working together building the house they lived in. The caption: *House built for Paul's arrival.*

The house was built into a hill with the back door opening at the top of hill and a view of the Rocky Mountains. The door on other side of the house opened at the street level. Paul was told by his mother and siblings that everything was because of him. They had a house, they now had more money, they all had to say he was their brother. His siblings would stay away from Paul as much as possible because everyone asked why he was so different. They ran away from him calling "You're not one of us."

Edna insisted that Paul was not allowed to be given the usual IQ tests. At school they agreed, as his brothers had achieved low standings. Paul was automatically placed in the special needs program, but the teachers noticed Paul spent limited time to finish all the activities and then helped others complete the work.

Paul was held back, like his brothers in first grade and was now finishing grade four as the school year was coming to an end. The school carried out tests to decide where all the students should be in the following year. Paul given the Mastery Test. The teacher argued with Paul on every answer he gave: "Are you sure that is level?"

Paul felt frustrated and asked, "Why do you want me to choose that position? That is not level, it's parallel." The teacher shook her head.

"This is wrong," she said. "You are completely different than your brothers. You don't belong in special needs at all."

"I don't," replied Paul.

There were more tests, and the school reported the results to Edna.

Paul noticed Edna sitting in her favourite easy chair in the front room as he got home on the last day of school in spring. She had her cup of water and the bottle of 222 pills beside her. She had arthritis and needed the drugs every day. She would be sleepy and speak with slurred words. She opened her eyes and said, "You're not my son."

Paul had heard this before but had said she was brought up as a Holdman Mennonite, they said that even if it wasn't true as a warning. He had to fit in with them, slow down, don't try so hard at school, she would explain.

"You weren't like your brothers, because I took you when you were born," she said.

"You told me that," said Paul. He had been told to not believe what she said when she was taking so many pills by his sisters, Julie, and Kate.

"I really didn't want another one like your brothers. When they were born the cried like a screeching cat. Now we must clear out of here because the school people are figuring it out," she continued.

Paul felt sick and afraid. There were empty cardboard boxes stack up by the back door. He went to the bedroom he shared with his brothers.

"This is all your fault," yelled Kate, Paul's sister. "I wanted to go to High School here, but now I must go to High Prairie. You proved in the tests you were different from us, and now we must move to the farm."

"I am completely different," said Paul.

"All that there is on the farm are uninsulated wood granaries we have to live in," Kate said.

"It gets cold in winter too," said Jonas. Their father had bought land on the Alder Ridge Road between High Prairie and Valleyview in the south Peace River region. "All we have is a wood stove to heat it, and that is where we have to go."

Paul felt bewildered and terrified. He had no idea how his test results meant they had to flee Hinton in summer.

After they moved Edna made arrangements at the school, so Paul had a position in the special needs program in grade five. He finished his year's schoolwork by the first week of October, as the year's content was presented in workbooks.

It was the beginning of the second week of October. The snow started to fall when the school bus brought Kate, David, Jonas, and Paul to the farm. The back of the station wagon was open, and boxes and suitcases were packed.

"Kate, Jonas, and Paul, you are coming with me. David's staying with your father," said Edna.

"We're leaving tomorrow morning for Altona, where your grandfather and grandmother are," said Edna.

"Well, that's better than staying here," said Kate. "Why are going there?"

"We'll just stay there until they help us set this place up," replied Edna.

Paul felt relieved as the four of them got into the station wagon. They travelled to Slave Lake and south to the Trans Canada highway and then east. The scene passed from early winter to late autumn and then to late summer as the travelled south.

Edna was preoccupied with family matters and had to find a job as a seamstress in a small facility in town. Paul was forgotten as he entered regular grade five class and made-up time lost in special needs. He had time at school and accepted his teacher invitation to make posters about people and history of Manitoba. His poster of Josiah Flintabbatey Flonatin, a cartoon character that the town of Fin Flon was named after brought students from other classes.

Classmates asked for Paul's cartoons, and he drew them. In a month Paul would sit in the school library drawing for other students. Paul was called *Wanda's boy* by his extended family and then other adults in the community. Edna was quick to say, "That's because you're an artist." Wanda, Paul's aunt had produced art and shared it with others. Paul marvelled at Wanda's drawings of Roman soldiers, Prairie Flora, perfectly inked flowers framed on the walls of his grandparents' house.

The spring came and the fields were in boom. Paul walked to the fields of sunflower and smelled the citrus earthy smell. He was happy and looked forward to summer in southern Manitoba.

Edna received what she came to Altona for, they packed and prepared to leave in summer. Jonas had another bad year in school and looked forward to returning to the farm. Kate and Paul felt dread as they watched the familiar town limits pass into the distance as they headed west.

*

Jenifer, Paul's wife agreed they had to find out if he had a different family. There was a sense of urgency, as Paul had swabbed his cheek and sent the sample for DNA test through a family heritage service. The results had arrived and there was some confusion, it showed family connection to his mother's side, but there was no connection to his father. Jenifer practiced family law and checked for documentary evidence.

Jenifer looked at Paul as he stepped inside the house at the end of the day. She smiled and hugged him.

"They called you Wanda's boy for a reason," she said.

"It wasn't because I was doing well in school and my art," replied Paul.

"No, there is no record of your birth at the Hinton hospital," said Jenifer.

"So, my birth certificate is false," replied Paul.

"Yes," replied Jenifer. "Wanda is recorded as giving birth to a baby boy on your birthdate at the Steinbech hospital. Your birth certificate was applied for through the Department of Vital Statistics, later, and it was issued. That was what it was like in those days." She paused, and then continued. "The DNA results make sense, Edna, was Wanda's sister, so all of the family members on the DNA site show up the same way for either of them."
"So, what about my father?" asked Paul.

"He's Harvy, Wanda's husband," Jenifer replied. "The DNA trail identifies those related to him. There is enough here to prove paternity in court."

"Did you find anything else?" asked Paul.

"Wanda died twenty-three days after you were born from complications of diabetes," she replied.

"I heard that when we lived in Altona," said Paul. "I didn't know when it happened."

"You had a brother, James," said Jenifer.

"Had?" asked Paul.

"He died of cancer," said Jenifer.

"James was my brother," said Paul. "I meant him several times when we were in Altona," said Paul. "He was friendly and nervous."

"Harvy died, but I couldn't find the cause," continued Jenifer.

There was no one to connect to, thought Paul. A sudden sadness was unexpected, until now the story had a distance to it.

Paul contacted Keren, and third cousin, through the family heritage service. She confirmed that Edna was not Paul's biological son. Dan, a third cousin, filled in a few details; none of Wanda's sibling got along. The greatest derision was directed at Wanda as she did well in school, had artistic abilities, and married Harvy, the town administrator in Steinbech.

Paul looked at the two stones he received from Mary. He placed them in a small white box with a photograph he downloaded from the internet of Wanda's and Harvy's graves. They were buried together.

Paul and Jenifer drove south and east toward Steinbech from Edmonton. The trip felt easy, as if they were being pulled toward something.

Jenifer stood with Paul looking at the Wanda's and Harvy's grave. The gentle breeze carried the smell of sage and sun flowers. Paul took the stone Mary had given to him and stepped toward the gravestone and kneeled carefully slipping it under the side. Paul tapped the gray stone until it couldn't be seen.

The Weight of What Goes Unspoken
Tinamarie Cox

The best *secret*-keepers
　　　are the ones who learned young.
Not to tell
anyone about the sorts of things that actually went on at home.
Not to talk
about any of their unimportant and inconvenient feelings.
Not to speak
about anything that didn't make their parents proud.

The *secret* was
we were all unhappy
　　　and we were taught to lie in smiles.
The *secret* was
we were not all that normal
　　　and made to believe love was supposed to hurt.
The *secret* was
　　　I struggled to live with all that weight.

And the most unspeakable *secret* of them all
　　　is that I nearly killed myself
　　　　　keeping all those *secrets* I wanted to share.

Home Is Where Your Mom Is

after Sierra DeMulder

Katie Hébert

I look out the 6th floor window of Mount Sinai and watch Central Park
Covered in smoke.
Tears strolling down the glass; Is this a mirror?
Echoing my face, rain and my mother's burning body
Swallowing this storm of a breaking tree.

My mother was born on February 18th, an Aquarius;
An air sign, fitting for how she's floating through life now
In a drawer there are old birthday cards and notes,
Tracing my mother's handwriting underneath skin,
I feel her ghost flip through pages.

Everyone has been telling me that she is in a better place,
Like she is #1 on God's guestlist,
His authority to take things from people that do not belong to him—
Just like this disease.
God must be a Cancer sign, born when the radiation is dangerous,
Or because Cancer is a water sign.
Water leaked in her brain,
Causing her to forget her own daughter's face—
Another broken organ.
I had to carry her to the stretcher because her feet could no longer touch the pedals,
All the keys playing hollow notes, everything out of tune.

My gynecologist asks about my family's history of cancer.
I tell her the recent loss of my mother,
And she lost her daughter the same way.
She presses down against my stomach, examining my uterus,
Waiting for another bond of birth to break under disease.
A wandering womb, old fashioned hysteria; that is how I must look to everyone.
This empty beating, this silent irony,
A child absent of protection,
Wandering aimless and empty and cold,
And everyone sees me hysterical and breaking.

I was an emergency c-section,
They broke into my mother's body to get me out.
Cancer broke into my mother's body to get her out.

My friend said that grief is like a brick in your pocket:
Heavy and hard, but you get used to carrying it.

My grandmother's house was built from the ground up only to be destroyed by a
hurricane.
When getting demolished, my mom wanted to keep a brick of it.
I am carrying her because God decided to send a hurricane into my family tree
Rip off a branch that didn't belong to him—
Typical of a Cancer to do.
And it is so typical of me, a Taurus, to be so stubborn,
To refuse this circle of life that demands my mother's body so soon.

Another poet says, "This, which is not at all beautiful nor poetic,"
Yet here I am, making my mother's death a perfect score;
Glorifying a soundtrack of nervous monitors and IV bags,
A chorus of doctors harmonizing that
there is
nothing
they
can
do.

At another person's house after a home-cooked meal,
I get handed a mug that reads
        Home is where your mom is
And I don't know where I go anymore.

Bored
Ana Martinez

I'm bored of being so leveled,
calm in crisis.
The hypertension diagnosis
came as a shock
considering how rarely my heartbeat
makes itself known these days.
Years of holding people's trauma
have taught me to dam my tear ducts,
shave my goosebumps,
restrain my shivers in cashmere sweaters
and lavender-scented scarves
         -    a therapist trick of the trade to regulate -
I'm tired of being so regulated.

I used to feel things.
Warm touches that melted
my anxiety ridden stiff upper lip,
tender tummy aches from tipsy laughing
during Christmas Eve dominoes.
Even my body's weight
when it collapsed on the kitchen floor
brought a morbid comfort
after reading her suicide note.

Now the work feels trite,
the tragedies predictable.
It is not natural to have a speech memorized
about how self-blame is a common response
to inexplicable pain,
because it gives us a sense of control.
        -    These sentences feel rote.

They say my compassion
is just a little tired,
my ambition burned out
somewhere along guiding people
in healing journeys.

I'm even bored
of these stupid heat metaphors,
How do I get out of it
without burning it all down?

Coma
Terry Sanville

For the second time, his blood glucose meter made a loud beeping sound. Chavez pulled his bicycle onto the country road's narrow shoulder and stopped. He fished the tiny black device from the rear pocket of his jersey; its screen flashed the number 55 followed by two arrows pointing downward.

How the hell did it drop twenty points, he thought. It's only been a couple minutes. He rummaged in the pocket for the bottle of cranberry juice that he always carried on his Sunday morning rides. The bottle was empty.

Great, low blood sugar and no carbs. I'm screwed.

He gazed along the road that wound over hills and across shallow valleys textured with vineyards to the distant outline of the city and home. The road stood empty of cars, too early for tourists to be up and about. Besides, the wine tasting rooms wouldn't open until eleven.

It's gotta be five or six miles to town. I can do this – stop at Dunkin' for a donut and juice. Better get moving.

Chavez mounted his skinny-tired bike and pushed off, pedaling slowly. A strong headwind made him select a low gear and climbing hills took his breath away. He pushed forward through what felt like glue, for what felt like forever. The horizon and the city seemed to draw no closer.

Should have stayed with Elliott, taken the coast route home. Stupid, stupid, stupid. Visions of his riding partner passing through quiet beach towns filled his mind. He shook his head to clear it and to focus on the way forward. His vision narrowed and his breathing increased, even when coasting downhill.

Chavez muttered to himself, "Come on, you can do this. Quit being a pussy, dammit. Count the strokes. That's it. That's it."

He looked down at his feet attached to the pedals going round and round, the road a blur of black asphalt. Then it changed to hard-packed earth. He raised his head and stared at the rutted track that headed into the coastal mountains, toward ranch buildings perched on ridgelines overlooking the valley. *What the fuck . . . how did I get here? I gotta stop.* But his legs were on autopilot and kept on pumping. He fumbled for his cell phone but it slipped from his trembling hands and disappeared. The pedals continued to spin. Black spots appeared in the centers of his eyes and the road became a tunnel leading toward a chaparral-covered slope. Someone turned a dimmer switch and the light faded. Then everything went to black.

*

Flap, flap, flap, flap, the sharp cracking sounds woke Chavez. He opened his eyes. Staring upward he watched the tent's ceiling pulse inward than snap outward in the high wind. He tried moving his stiff body, felt stabbing pains in his right hip. He lay on a cot near the partially opened entrance to the tent. Outside, clouds of dust streamed past. Men wearing camouflaged Army uniforms hustled by, heads bowed, facemasks pulled over their mouths and noses.

Sitting up, Chavez looked down at himself, decked out in a dusty uniform. Cots with footlockers and small tables holding personal items lined the tent's opposite wall. Men stretched out on their beds and snored in the oppressive heat. Chavez shook his head but the dream wouldn't clear. He stood, moved to the entrance and stared. The FOB (Forward Operating Base) looked like it had just been attacked. Black smoke mixed with dust blossomed upward from its far perimeter.

From down the road between the tents a lone soldier approached, M16 slung over a shoulder, helmet strap dangling. With shock and surprise, Chavez recognized his older brother, Daniel. Daniel walked toward him grinning and they fist-bumped, ducked into the tent and sat side-by-side on the cot. Daniel dropped his helmet onto the ground.

"Hey bro, shouldn't you be shuffling papers at the Command Center?"

Chavez forced himself to nod, still trying to wake from the dream. "Yeah, a whole lot of nothin' is going on out there."

"Nothing's good, real good."

"Yeah."

"So you wanna grab some chow?" Daniel stood, dust spilling from every fold of his uniform.

"Sure." What the hell is going on . . . Am I dead? Is this all some bogus dream?"

Groaning from exhaustion, the brothers stumbled along the road to the mess tent. They joined the chow line and were served fried chicken with white gravy, mashed potatoes and peas.

"Remember that time at the Forth of July party?" Daniel began.

"Sure do. Pop was roasting a half dozen chickens on the grill."

"Yeah, they smelled so damn good that we stole one and took it into the woods. Ate the whole thing."

Chavez laughed. "And we tried blaming it on Skeeter. That poor dog had those sad eyes that made him look guilty."

"But Pop wasn't buyin' it. It didn't help that we had chicken grease all over our T-shirts."

The brothers sipped bitter coffee lightened with fake milk and talked about the summers they'd ridden their bicycles for miles around their home city, talked about running away to the great north woods . . . but never did. They were only a year apart and did everything together, liked the same girls, hated school, fought often but always got over it.

Daniel had been the one who suggested they enlist in the Army – both had been out of high school and knocking about, taking any jobs they could find to pay for a shared apartment.

"Are you sorry you joined the Army?" Chavez asked.

"Not really. But I sometimes dream about me and Wells, escorting some convoy, him driving, Johnson riding shotgun, and me behind the M60. I think of IEDs and waking up dead. It's getting to me, Chavez. I hardly sleep anymore. I've started to go to church again. I'm praying a lot . . . doesn't seem to help." Daniel sighed. "But talking with you here, helps, ya know. Together, we can make it through just about anything."

Chavez stared into his brother's eyes and felt the fear radiate from him. He looked away, forcing images into his brain of childhood adventures, of how each brother looked out for the other. If someone tried to bully Chavez, they'd have both brothers to deal with.

A three-stripe sergeant came into the mess tent and motioned to Daniel.

"Sorry, bro. Gotta go. I'll see you."

"Yes . . . yes, I'll see ya. Be safe out there."

"Will do."

*

The cold wind washed across Chavez's face. The light came on slowly, gray at first then blinding white. He stared upward at a cloudless sky.

"He's coming back," a woman said.

"Come on, sit him up."

A man and a woman dressed in navy blue jumpsuits pulled him upright. "Do you know where you are?" the woman asked.

Chavez looked around. He sat on the side of a dirt road, his bicycle in the ditch, his arms and legs sporting angry road rash. "Yeah, I'm somewhere south of town."

"Do you remember how you got here?" the man asked.

"I was riding my bike. Had low blood sugar. Musta passed out."

"You're right. We've given you a shot of glucagon to bring you back."

Chavez gently rubbed the sore spot in the crook of his arm and covered by a bandage. He felt nauseated and sucked in deep breaths. He checked his glucose meter. It read 98 with double arrows now pointing straight up.

"Yeah, your sugar levels are going to bounce around a bit after that glucagon injection," the woman paramedic said. "Just keep track of it and don't give yourself too much insulin. You could get in trouble again if you do."

"Copy that," Chavez said. "Can I catch a ride into town with you guys?"

The male paramedic grinned. "We don't have room in the bus for a bike. But the Deputy Sheriff will take you home."

The conversation during the ride into town proved to be a clipped one.

"So you're a diabetic?" the deputy asked.

"Yeah, Type 1."

"You shoot up with . . ."

"Insulin. Yeah."

"My Uncle was a diabetic. He didn't last long."

"It runs in families," Chavez said.

"Just my luck . . ."

The deputy dropped him off at his apartment. For days, Chavez went to work and shuffled papers at the County Auditors Office. But the mental images of him and Daniel filled his private times. Their dream conversation had been so detailed but all too short. He wanted to tell more stories, to see his brother smile at each memory, to hear him laugh, watch him eat a meal – Daniel would never stop talking or close his mouth when eating, would never again worry about IEDs on that long road to Kandahar.

On Sunday, Chavez got up early and checked the air pressure in his bike's tires. He ate a light breakfast but took a larger-than normal dose of insulin. His blood glucose meter read 76 and falling when he left the apartment, double arrows down. Pedaling to the edge of town, he stopped at the small park near the base of a perfectly shaped hill. He found a bench next to the children's play area and sat. Only a few people were out that early, walking their dogs, the playfield grass still wet with morning dew. He sat and watched the sun cast shadows from the skeletons of the play equipment, across paths and grass, across empty streets and quiet homes.

His glucose meter beeped, signaling an accelerated downward turn. Chavez smiled and waited for the light to fade and that soft darkness to take him in. But before it did, he rummaged in his bike jersey, pulled a folded piece of paper from its pocket, and clutched it to his chest. He was ready now for another blast of Afghanistan's dusty wind and his dear brother, Daniel.

A woman walking her border collie noticed the middle-aged man slumped on the bench next to his bicycle. He didn't look like a drunk, was dressed in clean riding clothes, beard neatly trimmed, hair perfectly cut. He looked asleep, smiling, as if having a nice dream. She decided to leave him alone. But after walking a few yards, she turned and returned to his side. She shook him gently but he wouldn't wake up.

The paramedics arrived and checked his vitals, pulse barely there. They found his glucose meter – it read 32, double arrows down. They also found the scrap of paper he held tight. On it was written:

"Type 1 diabetic. I need glucagon. Bring me back so I can dream again."

A Lady Dying
Caitlin Jackson

There's a woman sunk into her rose armchair, velvet cushion imprinted by her timely ware, at the patterned wallpaper shell sit and stare the clock ticks and fills the air with time and space that's dusty and bare like the shelves and frames that lack purpose, just there, like the woman, empty of memory and deprived of care.

Her cup of tea is cold and leaves a bitter taste of neglect and rejection, it curdles to agraphobe with lumps of ache and burns her tongue through scorn and trauma. To sink it back and grimace is that of life to face after all it's plated up, the soggy cruelty consumed her, after being chewed up and spat out by those she loved and tried to provide for those she was good to. Her mother always said she was a good girl, placid, polite and considerate, whilst tugging her hair into ringlet pigtails or dragging her hand across the street. Submissive and scared, an automaton to past faces who stumped her and numbed her small heart.

 Her heart which sunk deeper than her body in her chair, she wishes she hadn't have cared, quite so much that it lead her through a life she didn't want and a life she can't bear, the life that lead her to this very armchair, like the bitter tea she pours and suffers through, because grief has stained her teeth and decayed her heart, just waiting for the day the clock stops ticking.

Quietness of sageness
Maja Zajaczkowska

I've been dreaming of cutting my tongue off for a few days now. I was walking through the streets of this misty, illusory town I was cursed to live in. I was thinking of how blessed it could be unable to speak. Not to bother anyone. Not to be bothered. It was awfully late at night; the time of the night when it was too late for the party and too early for the dawn birds to sing. I stopped next to the lantern and lit a slightly broken cigarette. Blue Camels, in a soft pack. Apparently a high-quality tobacco. The snow was falling on my face, drenching my tangled hair. My coat was soaking wet, and a small copy of Dazai's "No Longer Human" was hanging out of my pocket. It was damp with falling pages. Gramps would get me crucified for that, rest in peace.

I was walking back to my house, a place I sought some rest after doing absolutely nothing. Following the evening stroll, I usually sit in my beloved armchair. It once belonged to my grandfather. After a long day of work, this hallowed piece of furniture with navy blue upholstery and cigarette-burn holes was his favorite place in the house to rest. I never found out what he'd been doing for a living; nevertheless, it gave me an inheritance huge enough to never worry about having a job.

He used to sit down comfortably in his armchair, take one of the books from his library, and read till late at night. The library was the place I was allured mainly by. It smelled like old wood and bergamot tea, the dead flowers were arranged in the art deco vases, and dim light coming from an old kerosene lamp was embracing the room. Moonlight was lurking through red velvet curtains. His armchair was in the center, next to the small bureau always filled with notebooks, dip pens, inkwells, and porcelain teapots. He never allowed me to install an electric light there. He was firmly convinced that it damages the quality of books, (especially the old ones), or something like that.

Grandpa never talked too much; he believed conversations were a pestilence to the beauty of life. I vividly remember the moment he started speaking to me for the first time. One time I, a few years of age, sat by the leg of the armchair and timidly asked him to read me out loud the book he was currently holding on his lap. He looked at me with consternation and unnoticeably nodded his head. It quickly became our routine: every night he was sitting by the lamp and reading various texts to me. Shakespearean sonnets, Romantic poets, Russian existentialist novellas, Beckett, Wilde, Hemingway, Descartes, Plato, and many, many others.

As I grew older, he even allowed me to sit by the desk and take notes.

I strongly believed that introducing me to the world of literature was the only thing in the world that could make Papa content with his life. At times during his readings, when I couldn't understand a word or a meaning of the story and dared to ask him for an explanation, he always responded with a disdainful look, and, after a moment of silence, he continued to read. I quickly learned that if I ever wanted to get answers, I had to search for them in between those shelves myself.

I still recall his old pianist fingers scrolling through the yellowed pages, his sonorous voice uttering words out loud. The moment he opened the book we were conveyed into the realm of grand ideas and arcane stories. Those nights were only for us - a scarce ritual that provided an illusion of perpetual closure. A closure that wasn't obtainable during the daytime. That was only for both of us, half-asleep after the day of school and work, yet willing to sit in the sound of muted Mozart records, candlelight, and read for hours. "A still tongue makes a wise head. Remember that, boy.", he used to say. I can bet on my life that if it weren't for me and my little request he would take an oath of silence. I've been wondering for a long time if he ever had any affection for anyone. That was until Grandma died.

The sound of honking cars woke me up from my memories. I was playing with a small clasp knife in my left hand, musing on whether it was possible to bleed to death from my mouth. My hands got purple-red from the cold. A woolen scarf was tightly knotted on my neck, making it almost impossible to breathe. That reminded me of my early school years when I eagerly avoided speaking up. The only person I spoke to was Grandpa, during our evenings. And even then I tried to speak not as much, not because I didn't want to, but because I did not wish to make him upset. When I got older and learned how to read, I tended to think about the importance of uttered words. Although he was immensely wealthy, Grandpa constantly repeated that the only richness in life that matters can be gained through literature (well, that was partly true. The other half of my wealth I owe his will). Once I discovered that books can provide me with everything I need, I never worried about my social life.

I stared at the lamp, and for a few minutes watched snowflakes spinning around the streams of light. Neons of local stores were flashing in front of my eyes, blurring the sight of well-trodden paths of snowy streets. There wasn't anyone outside, which gave me a sense of timorous safety. I started sweating under the layers of shirt, sweater, and woolen coat. As I was walking in between dark avenues I began considering the pros and cons of the absence of the tongue in my mouth. Let's say that, hypothetically, it will be cut off and I will survive.

The seeds of wondrous possibilities of what I could gain from this were already deeply rooted in my consciousness.

*

"Then he cut out the tongue of that godless man, promising to feed it bit by bit to the birds and to hang up his head opposite the Temple, as evidence of what his foolishness did for him." 2 Maccabees 15:33.

'Maybe I am foolish for the plans of self-laceration. I ought to listen to the Holy Bible. Follow sacred words. Seek redemption. But if a man was created in the image of God, so within the injury, I ultimately hurt the Almighty. Maybe I'm godless for such thinking. Foolish thinking. A godless fool.', I thought while turning the key in a door. If I deprived myself of an organ responsible for speaking, I would have no business exposing myself to the world again. I wouldn't cause any pain to people, and myself. And if I tried, nobody would even care enough to learn sign language for me, me included.

"I'd rather be mute than mumble nonsense all the time, which most people do nonetheless.", Grandpa said to me one December night, shortly before Christmas.

"But what if something happened to me, and I needed to ask for help?"

"Oh, dear, don't be so naive. Anyone would rather choose ignorance than help you. Humanity is selfish in its core.", he said in his calm, hollow voice, and came back to his lecture.

He was reading Kafka's "The Trial" that evening.

I think I should blame my grandfather for not having any friends. My parents weren't around since I was born, so both of my grandparents volunteered to raise me. My grandpa knew from an early age that I was a loner, and he did not hesitate to change that; better, he embraced my love for solitude. I was a quiet kid in school, to the point that when I decided to open my mouth, it was such a shock to my colleagues that I quickly became a subject of ridicule. The more they laughed, the more I laughed with them, and the more anxious I became.

I entered the house and put the kettle on. The intrusive thoughts were haunting me again.

What would happen if I just shut up?

Grabbed the knife from the shelf. It was so close, a few centimeters from my face the liberty, freedom of non-speech! Salvation in the form of eternal silence! How blissful it could be! How emancipating…benedictio Dei…what was I doing? I put the knife down and instantly felt embarrassed. Child play. The thought of him being disappointed with me threw shivers down my spine.

Who do I think I am? Some sort of modern, facetious martyr? A low-brow version of

Christ?

Suddenly the phone rang in the living room. I rushed through the hallway, still wearing my wet coat. I left a track of water behind me.

"Hello?"

"Hi, is this James?" a female voice asked, or rather screamed. She sounded like a screeching cat at dawn. Maybe she was one of Grandpa's old friends. Not many people knew he killed himself right after Grandma passed away, and they often called to ask how he was doing.

"Yes, what is it?"

"It's Bethany here. I'm just calling to check on your grandpa. How is he doing? He hasn't phoned me in months. Is he locked in his office?"

"Yes."

"With all those dusty books, I suppose?"

"You know how it is, he still processes grandma. He never goes out of his room", I replied as calmly as I possibly could. I didn't want this stranger to catch my voice cracking.

"Oh honey, you have to tell him to knock it off! It's been almost five years now!", the voice began sounding progressively more and more irritating.

"I'll pass this to him, thanks.", I said and hung up.

I marched back into the kitchen. Once I passed my grandfather's office, I couldn't help myself but step in. I hadn't been there once since his passing, so the dust gathered on those shelves and the bureau made me cough intensely. Still thinking about this screeching lady, I approached the desk. His last letter was lying there, as if he still was considering leaving me.

'Please forgive me, son, though I wanted to remain in everlasting silence…' I noticed his letter knife next to the lamp.

'…and taken to the Heavens above…'

I picked it up and took a closer look; the handle was made from a hard, madly expensive wood. He always valued high-quality craftsmanship. The freshly sharpened blade still remembered the touch of his warm wrists. There were a few drops of dried blood on the edge. '…where by the side of my beloved ones, I shall find peace.'

I knew the content of the note by heart now, yet I never dared to hide it anywhere or even touch the surface of the paper. As if leaving all his belongings as they were could bring him back. The one thing I can blame books for is that they made me sentimental. A difficult, foolish romantic. I put the knife next to my tongue and looked at my reflection in the mirror. My eyes were empty, looking for some absolute truth; the only path that can lead me to redemption. Forgetfulness for not helping him, for letting him bleed to death on this chair while I was peeking through the keyhole.

I couldn't do anything. I had to respect his silence. To fix everything….I could fix everything…This, I thought, could fix everything.

The snow was placidly dancing behind the glass as if nature was preparing me for what was yet to come. I put the knife closer and smelled the bitter metal.

A still tongue makes a wise head. I'm foolish enough to pursue wisdom.

Blood spilled on the letter, soaking in the wood underneath it. It covered every word written on the paper.

It's Too Late Once The Toadstools Explode
Michael Cunliffe

I stood – bereft of sense – hugging you in the hallway,
Your smart phone a half-bounce from your right foot
Sheathed in an off-white, scuffed Dunlop Volley
I'd bought online for your birthday last year.
They didn't quite match your new black Gymshark leggings
Or your pastel pink Lorna Jane workout singlet.
You didn't cry. In months to come I would often wonder why.
You stood there, eyes bare, a deep stare into slow-moving air,
Breathing barely. My arms wrapped – so full of care –
Tight around your torso, pleading, pleading, *feel my despair*
As your limp arms languished by your side.

I'd bought a pair of leather low-top sneakers, Adidas or maybe Puma,
I can't recall. Women's U.S. size 7,
Cali-style, white with chrome-stripes.
An online shopping impulse-buy, and
I thought for sure you were gonna love them.
They were, "for you". They were, "just coz".
With free express delivery for online purchases over $150.

I couldn't have known your father would pass away
The very next day. Right in his lane, a stroke
At the bowling alley. His third strike in a row, then
Sixty seconds later...
How could I know?
That's not how it was supposed to go.

Two days later the package arrived by courier.
I'd forgotten it was coming. I was silent. I didn't know what to say.
In a cupboard I tucked it away. I feared your thoughts,
The tears, the words that may follow.
That perhaps I was trying ease your pain with sneakers.
So I stayed silent. Drifted through nothingness,
Bringing you cups of tea as you slouched on a back patio chair,
Eyes bare, staring idly at slow-moving air,
Thick, grumbling thunderclouds of white cigarette waft
Dissolving into space as the monochrome words
Of a funeral eulogy barely heard by tear-stained ears.

For days and days we did not speak. You never got angry.
You never screamed and wailed and raged and cried,
Thumped your fist on the kitchen bench and cursed god.
Do something, tell me to fuck off or something.

I didn't know what to say.
So I continued to sink in steaming teacup silence,
Bobbing up and down, a sapped ginger and lemon herbal infusions teabag.
I felt discarded. I felt drained. Day by day
Your eyes never settled on me for more than a few seconds.
"Are you okay" – "Are you coping" – "What's your favourite memory" –
Questions never marked in our grim silence,
My mind desperately grasping, grasping for a foothold, for a first word,
My mind slipped again and again on the silence that grew around us,
Creeping as mildew across our skin, our lips, our eyes
Then bursting overnight as a toadstool from our nothingness,
Over and over, night after night, by the thousand
Bursting, ballooning toadstools of silence exploding
Chaotically, morning after excruciating, dew-glistening morning.

I feel such a fool. One word – one exasperating, invisible word –
I don't know what it was, I never found it.
It sounds so stupid, I know. That one cat hair floating on air,
The more I snatched at it, the further from my hand it drifted.
What you must think of me now, it haunts me as I toss and turn at night.
We are one-hit wonders two years after hitting the charts.
I look back and I can't remember ever speaking another word.

I remember the silence. The silence of your packing
As your seagull on the horizon eyes lingered sidewards of me.
The silence of your last coffee, your last cigarette.
The silence of your car pulling out of the driveway.
The silence of the sneakers that arrived via courier
Now in the bedroom, our walk-in robe,
The left-hand side now bare except for the top shelf.
Still sitting there, unmoved, the unopened box,
Dust creeping as mildew across the undisturbed lid
Reminding me of all the things I never said.

No, because
Syreeta Muir

Will I ever speak to you about the situation abroad and then,
in the next breath, mention the beauty of your name?
Not me. I used to get blamed for breaking things at school
—brown hands, prone to mischief,
I always get caught.
I was a funny child. I learned that round at a friend's house;
that I was funny, clumsy.
Not smart, though too clever for my own good.
I can tell you are confused. Me too.
Want to know which country I am from?
Who is my real mum?
Can my cold hands ask your warm heart
such things?
No, because
they can only give you a hot take
on the length and ache of the river Avon.
How careful you and I are learning how to be.

A Food Diary of the Week You Left
Stephanie Axley-Cordial

Monday: your mother's flavorless ham and cheese casserole from when our son was
born, freezer burned
still cold in the middle.

Tuesday: The slice of wedding cake
we forgot to eat on our first anniversary.

Wednesday: Tinder and Bumble with a side of
catfish and my dignity.

I wish you would clean your own plate.
So many ways my body, my size
could be your prize at the apocalypse of our ode.

Emptied of your hot air, gas lit for flash
I surrendered to the weight of your
Consuming oblivion.

The last time you called me beautiful, you were grabbing my tits with an
arrogance of ownership.
I thought
I owed you
I cried when
we fucked trying to make love, again.

No longer your vessel, the packhorse for your shame, I now know I came to you with a
question never yours to answer.

Thursday: my pride and the strawberries from
the first garden.
You only called me fat once in the way that was beyond an adjective
the slur amplified by the case of Natty Light.
I always mistook your words as nourishment.

Friday: the final watered down
bottle of booze
"My body! my choice!" you declared,
appropriating my most painful memory, as a shield to your disease.
I grieve through a credit card worth of takeout.

Saturday: the Chinese place
you would never try
and a deep breath.

Strong back- in. Soft front- out.
I go to the bakery for hardware.
I make my own bread now.

Sunday: one ripe peach.

Metanoia

Barbara Meier

change in one's way of life resulting from penitence or spiritual conversion.: "what he
demanded of people was metanoia, repentance, a complete change of heart".

I lay in hypnopompic sleep,
expiring the night air and inhaling the morning breath,
moist and sweet with manzanita blooms and wild lilac blossoms.
I feel the body next to me, warm, alive, breathing,
and at that moment, so real and vibrant,
we are one again.
The birdsong is a lullaby of metanoia,
memories of when we made love in our marriage bed,
nestled under the wool comforter.
But the dreamlet fades,
as does the bird song.
I wake to brassy daylight
bearing down through my window.
I reach for one last embrace and find myself clutching sheets.
There is no reconciliation with the dead,
just a ghost sleeping in my bed.

To this day, we still refer to the empty bottles and beer cans as bodies.
Christopher Martinez

One day, towers fell and kids we once knew were off to war.
We had our bootheels dug into Central Texas–
could only get loose when a cold one was cracked open,
and we cracked open.

Like a war, we understood both blood and wine love to be emptied.
Like a war, we'd reach the bottom of blood and wine with more questions and no
answers.

We drank when the kids we knew didn't come back.
We drank when they did.
We drank when we saw a touchdown, a pretty girl, or a paycheck–

Night after night,
we climbed into these bottles as if they were bomb shelters
and held on to the next person as if they were bulletproof–

The bodies piling up in the corners of the fields.

Around here, it's all we have.

Thank God they're over there
keeping us so very free.

Arctic Star
Kim Gravell

"We took to the lifeboats," he said. "Those of us that could."

His hands, holding the box of matches, shook.

"There was nothing else for it. We all knew she was going down. Everything was burning; the ship, the water, the men in it." He swallowed convulsively. "Poor sods, not that they stood a chance anyway. You went overboard in those waters you were dead in two minutes from the cold.

"When the boilers went up, that was it. We were away by then but those that weren't – well, the explosion broke her back and down she went taking anyone left on board with her. Unnatural, it was, her rudder and prop up in the air like that, silhouetted against the sky…" His voice tailed off and I knew he was seeing again that ill-fated merchantman, frozen in the moment before she slid beneath the Arctic waves.

"There were too many in our lifeboat; too many and so badly hurt. Burns and blast injuries like I'd never seen before and hoped to God I'd never see again. We had no way to help them. We dropped them over the side one by one as they died. There was nothing else we could do." The white scars on the backs of his hands tightened and bunched as his fists clenched.

"We were adrift for five days before we were picked up. The convoys had orders not to stop for survivors, see. It was more important that they got through with their supplies. A handful of lives against the fate of a nation? Well, there's no contest. It was harsh but we knew the score when we signed on. We even joked about it. On your last night in port your mates would come aboard and go through your things. 'You don't need a change of clothes 'cos you'll be torpedoed first night out,' they'd say before making off with your spare shirts and anything else they fancied. We all did it.

"It was a trawler out of Nova Scotia that found us. Six men out of a full crew; the only ones who made it. When we got home the paper took our pictures, standing on the quayside in the clothes the Sally Army had given us. They said we were heroes, but we weren't; we were just lucky. I was seventeen.

"It was years before I could go out on November the Fifth. All those rockets … when you've seen it for real, the shells and the flares, it's not something you play at for enjoyment. You don't want reminding, it's there every time you close your eyes." He shook his head as if to dislodge the memories and come back to the present. "Ah, but it was a long time ago, pet."

His hands steady once more, he struck the match, holding it to the touchpaper and, as together we watched the rocket blossom in the sky, I marvelled at how far my father had come.

The Weight of it All
Ifrah Yousuf

First attempt: Baggage Weight = 3000 pounds

I try to pack 24 years of life into two hard-sided pink and brown suitcases, filling every nook and cranny till the bags are bursting. I'm confronted by their weight limit. I understand that airlines have their rules but how do they expect me to shrink down my room to a mere 160 pounds? How do I pick what comes with me on this new journey and what gets left behind? Should I pack the essentials or the sentiments? How do I pack the memories of my first kiss in this room, my first heartbreak, or my first panic attack? I don't even know what essentials I would need. I have never lived on my own. Although the excitement to move out of this crowded room and have the freedom to do whatever I want with no restriction is eclipsed by the anxiety to figure all of this out within a week and travel seven seas from everything I have ever known.

Second attempt: Baggage Weight = 1200 pounds – Four walls removed.

Is there a way I can sneak people through the security checkpoints? I need the people who helped me create those memories that I hold so close to me. I don't see eye to eye with my mom in most matters. She is one of the main reasons I have been working so hard to make sure I can leave this house after I complete my undergraduate. But she is also the reason I have made it so far. She fought against every societal taboo thrown our way since my father passed away and provided for us to the best of her ability with the resources she had. Who would I look up to for courage when the crushing weight of societal expectations will push me to surrender? My siblings and I have often fought like Tom & Jerry but whenever it's us against the world, we become family, like the one Vin Diesel cherishes in Fast & Furious. Who would stand up for me when someone is bullying me there? After a lot of bad luck in friendship, I finally found Saboor and Zunair who have stayed on a call with me when I am having a panic attack. They surprised me at midnight with a cake on my birthday. How will I find people like them again? And if I did, would I be able to trust them? I don't know if I can get that lucky again.

Third attempt: Baggage Weight = 440 pounds – Five people removed.

The shells of the suitcases strain against the small library of books they contain. Each book has a story associated with how they came into my life. Some I found, while others found me. When everything in my life was going wrong, I knew I could escape to a new world with just the flip of a page. What will I turn to in a foreign world where I don't know anyone and I stay cooped up in my room? Sure, I can get new books, but it will not have the same smell of home or the spine break from when I couldn't find a bookmark and have to leave it upside down.

Fourth attempt: Baggage Weight = 240 pounds – 185 stories removed.

I look at all the clothes, art supplies, sketchbooks, bedroom décor, journals and spices that lie at the bottom of my suitcases. After researching the weather of the place, none of my clothes will be the right fit for weather that cold. How will I express my individuality if I can't wear the real me? The art I have been practising for years has to be left behind. There is no time and place for a hobby that doesn't pay the bills. Anything associated with even a shred of emotion has to stay back in this room, if they come with me, I won't be able to focus on my mission. The mission to be the first unmarried woman in the family to start a life abroad. The mission to help my family climb up the social class ladder. The mission to prove that I am not a failure. And the only way I can do this is by leaving behind my heart - and my baggage - in this room.

Last attempt: Baggage Weight = 160 pounds – Emotions removed.

yoga woman arching from your bed

MaryAlice Dixon

of pain
and weathered pine
bridging
from a fallen plank
your body splinters
into sage
and silver thyme
shedding
skin in the acid rain
of cancer
crutch and cane

you rise
taking with you
not the baggage
of your body
but the lightness
of your breath
a breeze
that temples in a tree

The Price I paid for baggage with a learning disability
Michelle Steiner

Disabilities come with baggage that you pay a hefty price for. I have carried the baggage of having a learning disability since Kindergarten. The cost of these parcels has been frustration, shame, doubt, and anxiety. I wanted to throw the luggage away and break free. The strong heavy weight held me back. To move forward I had to take out each piece of luggage and weigh the cost.

Frustration was the heaviest cost of having a disability. My irritation of not being able to learn simple concepts in kindergarten, such as counting and tying my shoes, was apparent. My teachers saw that I could not master these concepts and I was visibly upset. The school recommended that I be evaluated for having a learning disability. I had to repeat the grade the following year in a different school and began to receive specialty instruction and accommodations. Having the different type of instruction helped me to learn because my brain needed alternative strategies. The accommodations of having extra test time, and having the test read aloud was prescribed to give my brain extra time to process information and be able to function outside of learning support.

Using services in another school added to the weight of shame. I attended school in a small conservative district. The school community was one where everyone knew each other and was close knit, if you fit in. I could not hide the fact that I had to go to learning support for classes. Everyone could see it! My peers knew where I received instruction but were not aware of what went on in the classroom. Many of them thought that I got the answers or did simple work. Many of them began to bully me by excluding me and saying unkind words. I felt ashamed for having one and wished my disability would go away. For years I was hesitant to tell others that I had one, for fear of rejection. I tried to break away from the baggage, but it continued to follow me. Having one stuck out like a bright pink luggage tag, alongside khaki, and black luggage.

Doubt was another substantial cost of the baggage. I doubted that I could learn or have success in my life. As a young child I thought that life would always be difficult. I thought what the point was of putting in the work, when all I was going to do was fail. I can remember studying for tests and failing them. I also recall the effort that I put into classes and not doing well in them. I doubted that I could be successful.

Anxiety was also another sturdy weight. I would be anxious at the start of each school year, wondering if I was going to have understanding teachers. I also feared that I would pass each year, because of failing kindergarten. I remember my learning support math teacher in middle school, telling me that there was no learning support math in high school and telling me to sign up for basic math class. I spent all summer worrying about it and I struggled in class. The teacher did not know what to do with me and it turned out there was learning support math. I was placed in the other class that had math on my level.

I also had the fear of not graduating high school, even though my grades were good. When school staff would talk about students not graduating, I took it to heart. I knew that failure could happen, and did not want to experience that again.

I carried the anxiety of not being able to do well when I was in college. I wondered if I could handle it with having one. I was not alone in my fears of higher education. My learning support teacher did not think that I could manage it because of my math skills. She suggested trade school instead. I had a psychiatrist who thought that I would not go beyond community college. Once I got to college, I had an advisor who told me that I would have limited job choices. I also had professors who told me that I was a bad writer.

I have experienced anxiety in employment. I have feared making mistakes or not being able to perform at the job because of my disability. When I told others of my fears other people would dismiss my concerns saying that it would not happen. I have had jobs where I did indeed fail, despite trying my hardest., I was fired by a few employers for making too many mistakes and simply not being able to learn the job. I had an employer who thought that I made the mistakes on purpose and tried to take away my unemployment.

My dreams often seemed like a lost piece of luggage at baggage claim. I watched as other people got their bag of knowledge and led fulfilled lives. I spent so much time focused on watching other people get their parcels, that I almost missed my own! My own success and power were right in front of me. My bag of success did not look like everyone else's. I had to work harder, use different resources and support. Despite all my efforts I may not be able to fulfill every dream that I want and have some tasks that I simply cannot do. The bag that I have had some rips, holes and dents in throughout out the years. Wear and tear is another price I paid for this parcel.

Carrying this bag cost me a heavy price, but it has shaped me into the person I am today. I have turned the pain of having one into one of purpose. Today I get to help others with disabilities to feel empowered and connected. I work as a para educator where I help students with not only their schoolwork but also to learn how to be an advocate for themselves. I also get to connect with others with my blog called Michelle's Mission. If I did not have a disability I don't know if I could truly be empathetic towards others. Having one has made me into the person that I am today.

I will never be able to fully take off the baggage of having a disability. Forever I will carry this accessory with me, but the bag has gotten lighter. I have learned how to deal with frustration by simply surrendering and accepting that there are some things I cannot change. I chose to focus on the things in life I can change and do well at. I feel empowered when I engage in activities that I love and can be successful with. The shame that I once felt for having a disability has also slowly faded. I now have confidence to say that I have one and to share my story. I also no longer doubt that my disability will hold me back in life and I will not be successful. I will have setbacks and failures, but I also know that I also have success and accomplishments. The anxiety has also lifted as well. I may not always have understanding people or the right accommodation, but I know how to work through demanding situations. The baggage will always be a part of me, but it no longer weighs me down. I can now move forward and into a brighter and lighter future.

My Rock
Mandy Prell

My story - more accurately - the experience that happened, is a rock.
A rock that, like a tumor, is welded to the curves of my brain, bulging up against the
interior of my skull: a permanent souvenir of my experience.

A woman wants to rip out my rock and show it to the world.
It will be empowering, she says, to put it on display for all to see and, without
permission, she performs brain surgery.

A doctor explains what the rock is.
She has studied rocks, she says. She tells me what I am experiencing and, without
permission, she writes off my rock in the form of a prescription.

A politician uses my rock.
I fight for you and beside you, he says, weaving a garish blanket with his words and,
without permission, he canvasses my rock.

A friend rejoices in my news; she has a rock too, she says!
She cannot wait to show me her rock and compare it to mine and, without permission, she
exchanges our rocks.

My mother holds a funeral for me and my rock.
She demands an open-casket service; wails so that everyone can see how she grieves and,
without permission, she says that the rock is really hers.

My co-workers are embarrassed by my rock.
Lazy, late, and always ill, they say, it interferes with their productivity and ambition and,
without permission, they mock my rock.

The experience that happened.
The experience that happened to me.
The experience that happened with me in it.
The experience that happened and happened again.
The experience that doesn't define me but is a part of my brain.
The experience that is not an excuse or a ploy or a lie or a dream.
The experience that is a rock and, like a tumor, is welded to the curves of my brain.
Not your rock.
Not his rock.
Not her rock.
Not their rock.
My rock.
My rock that weighs me down.
My rock that I carry.
My rock that hurts.

Leg Clips
MaryEllen Shaughan

My husband applied the clips to my legs early in our marriage; it was something everyone did, he said. And what did I know? I was young; a small clip on the outside of each leg was not a problem. I just had to be sure to dry them well after showering – we didn't want them to rust. Occasionally, I would feel an itch, but when I went to scratch, I had trouble locating the source of my discomfort; then the bell on the dryer would chime, letting me know it was time to fold the laundry, and I would forget all about it.

Over time, I nearly forgot about the clips. My husband certainly knew more about the real world than I did. I was, after all, just a house wife, as they used to call us. My job and only job was to take care of the house and our five children. My husband's thoughts were my thoughts; his opinions were my opinions. Until they weren't. Until one day he said,

"We've grown apart, and I have fallen in love with a supervisor at work. I will support the children, but you will need to get a job."

Job? I already had a job. I was a mother. A mother with no education, no other job qualifications. So I decided to go to college – me, a middle-aged, not-so-smart-woman with clips on her legs. Because I could think of nothing else, I studied what I thought I might like: chemistry, botany, astronomy, geology. And discovered that I was better than not-so-smart.

Every day was a surprise, especially the day the chemistry professor passed back last week's exam, showing that I had missed one question only. I read the question again, then re-read my answer. Though I could feel my insides turn to jelly at the thought, I was so certain of my answer that I brought it to the attention of the professor. He hemmed and hawed, and finally agreed that, yes, I was correct. I, the middle-aged, not-so-smart-woman with clips on her legs had earned 100 on a chem exam. And then, I heard two loud snaps; when I looked down, I saw that the clips on my legs had popped open, and my legs were growing, growing; soon, I was towering over my professor. And then I felt a long-forgotten itch, and turned my head just in time to see small stubs of wings sprouting from the shoulders of my cotton housedress.

Closet Makeover
Diane Funston

The skeletons are gone now.
Evicted after rent control failed,
moves across country,
across the Golden State,
in and out of disparate lives
hardly recognizable now.

The young poet, when poets
dressed the part. Velvet
cloak and flowing dresses
floated in enigmatic twirls
in smoky coffee houses
now gone, most likely gentrified.

The student, carved leather
ponytail holders, Indian gauze
peasant blouses, scent of
patchouli deep in creases,
t-shirts of musicians,
earth-born shoes,
and book bag stuffed with ego.

The mom, also cross-dressed
with student and worker
with developmentally disabled adults.
More t-shirts,
some stained, logos faded,
jeans as uniform,
earrings and necklaces left off
or pulled off those days.

The case manager, office job,
dress pants and serious tops,
blazers and sensible dress shoes.
Never comfortable in an office,
confused with Excel spreadsheets
and billable time. Fortune smiled,
laid off after six months, two years
unemployment checks arrived.

Aging became more noticeable too,
at first covered by monthly chemicals,
my hair whitened into the blizzard

I now wear proudly. My clothing
colors too, from favorite green
to royal blue to enhance my ermine crown.

Now, comfortable clothes
without pretense or uniform.
In this pandemic time,
making sure top half presentable
for Zoom groups of new friends,
chapters and verse
from far away and close.

If this is indeed the new norm,
I could do with just a weeks' worth
of clothes, donating my closet
to others to try on for size.
I putter in my garden,
I putter with words, play with
my dogs and hike with my husband,
less dressed to kill
and much more dressed to live.

Vespers
Raymond Luczak

Though my shoulders are sore from carrying the load of my days, though my sandals have chafed into the tender joint between toes, though my fingers are white-knuckled from swinging the weight of memory in a flimsy plastic bag, though my chest is atlassed with continents of sweat, though my belly rumbles forth the thunder of hunger, though my knees yelp from the fingersnaps of pain, though my lower back feels the pinch of agony, though my eyes are watery with misery, though my glutes ache for deep massage, I shall nevertheless raise up my face and sing a song, for you, wafting through the dank prison of my soul, bring the key of sunlight that frees me from the darkness of my days. Night in your bed shall come like myrrh and frankincense, and dawn in your arms shall resurrect my soul for another day of hard roads. I will always rise.

The Empty Corners of My Suitcase: Minimalism in Travel
Elizabeth Morelli

"What's this?" The security agent at Dulles Airport rubs the two drawstrings of my cargo pants between her purple latex fingers as if asking for an anatomical correction.

"Tie for my pants," I answer and then realize why she ushers me aside after the body scan. My black cargo pants have three zippers and metal-tipped ties all in the pelvic area. According to my friends, the perfect travel pants are loose yoga, but cargos have that rough-hewn travel look, a little more formal than the yogas in which I often sleep.

I am exacting about my travel choices, and confiscation of pants before I board a flight is nerve-racking. My small red carry-on contains one pair of jeans, khakis and one pair of capri pants for eight days of travel. If they confiscate the cargos, will they keep them, or return them, so can I wear them again in Budapest, my first central European city on this trip? My travel things, which may sit in drawers for months when I'm home, become my go-to crutches when each trip begins, and airport security becomes their first obstacle. The beginnings go deep. I traveled to New Mexico four days after 9/11, and stupidly brought a Swiss army knife and cuticle scissors with me. I said good-bye to my possessions in Norfolk, Virginia before boarding. Talking in staccato sentences, the security guard mentioned that the cost of the knife and the scissors was a minor blow to the budget when up against a trip to the southwest. But I felt guilty, dirty even, responsible for all the national catastrophes of the year due to "inappropriate packing." The two sentence lecture and confiscation—and escorted out of line—reminded me that I could be back in elementary school and caught sneaking a piece of soft art clay home breaking the art teacher's rules and putting the class's clay project in jeopardy.

To pack to get through airport security is dicey and add to that the complexity of electronic devices. The day before my central European trip, I removed my PowerCore mini charger from my backpack realizing it contained a lithium battery and needed to be packed in checked luggage. A friend had suggested I buy the battery because it was the perfect answer to keeping the charge on the idevices for an extra ten hours. When the charger arrived, the UPS driver placed the Amazon box on one of my steps, not even on the porch, possibly because of the huge red warning for the lithium battery inside. Ironically, the lithium battery was plane worthy in the cargo section, but not in my backpack—and I do not check luggage anymore.

My possessions need to be close to me on a trip—and minimal. I want to move fast once on the ground, darting down airport ramps to public transportation. Several years ago, I checked my last suitcase on a journey to Iceland. The ultimate prize was a boat trip from Reykjavik to see the Northern Lights. A bulky jacket, scarf, boots, mittens, hunter's socks filled the 25-inch suitcase crevices. I was ready. Reykjavik turned tropical that first week in March. People shed their outerwear—and no Northern Lights appeared for the full six nights. My best travel decision was adding a swimsuit for the geo-thermal waters of the Blue Lagoon. The wasted packing played heavily on my perception of that Iceland trip, so the following year, I packed a simple carry-on for an eleven-day trip to the

Canary Islands. When the Islands turned unexpectedly cold and rainy, I purchased a thin and compliant thrift store scarf. Bundled up with my four-foot scarf, I sat on a bench reciting *less is more* until I could take the emphasis off my cold toes. Weighing the two experiences, cold toes and the carry-on won out along with a carry-on preference.

Before I left on this recent trip, a well-meaning friend insisted that a bulky converter was what I needed for charging appliances in Central Europe. From previous trips I thought I needed an adapter, and the converter would only be necessary if not dealing with 110v or 220v, but he kept shouting travel guru "Rick Steves" name, and I allowed that reference to dictate my choices. When I arrived, I found that European hotels use a 220-voltage switch and that takes a simple plug-in adapter, not a converter. Since I didn't have the adapter in Budapest, I was sent to an Apple iPhone friendly café with charging capabilities, while in Prague the hotel desk clerk held up the adapter as if a magic seed that would grow into a much-needed beanstalk. It did.

The same friend mentioned that they had taken Tram 22 for a full circle around Prague, so on a rainy day, after a visit to the Castle, and missing my connection, I jumped on Tram 22 clasping the detailed email and assumed I could look at all of rain-drenched Prague in the rotation. Ninety minutes later I was at a terminus station somewhere in the far east end. The conductor used hand gestures to tell me "The End," On returning home, the friend admitted that he might have misquoted a *Lonely Planet* travel book this time. Travel pages, now Google maps, trump personal recollection.

Copies of city maps, emails and reprints of travel book pages are always in my backpack, but when trying to negotiate an exact street corner at a crucial moment, it is easier to ask— and most of my questions seem to involve directions and public transportation. Counting stations helps with the language barrier as does keeping the country's exact change for bus/subway in my right pocket (or available credit card for swiping), but I seldom, if ever panic, when I wander through a city with no sense of who I am/where I am. I grew up in an attic bedroom a flight of stairs and a closed door away from my family, and when the night turned overly dark, I told myself that morning was seconds away, and I would count until the numbers or dark ran out. Once in Rome I was in a hotel in the complicated Campo de' Fiori medieval district when I decided to explore and buy dinner in the process, so I walked quite a distance within the labyrinth of walls, without awareness or street names, until a pizza place popped up. After I bought a pizza slice, I asked how to get back to the Hotel Albergo. The clerk used hand signals, a rough sketch, and street names to lay out a complicated route. I managed the first few blocks of the directions, then stopped in a café for a drink and asked again. Another few blocks gained. Finally, a cannolo pastry brought me to a square adjacent to the hotel—with the bagged dinner intact. The process has never failed, and I still own the pizza clerk's rough map.

Though I have minimized my suitcase contents, I still hoard paper travel items. Duplicate copies of boarding passes, cruise tickets, parking passes, emails, copies of travel book pages all in order of date (and paper-clipped by color for area) fill up much of the backpack. Yes, there are phone apps to prevent the avalanche of paper tickets, but I worry about the phone's charge and capability when I need to produce proof of boarding immediately. Standard recycled (30%), bright white paper never fails, except when I misplace sheets (usually out of chronological order) or throw one away at the wrong stop.

As a trip progresses, and I check-off the cities, I toss the sheets and penned ideas to leave a little room in my carry-on for whatever I bring back—a mound of receipts, a small toy or two for the kids, a tiny Christmas ornament from each location— souvenirs that I don't really want but feel obliged to carry to provide evidence of the experience. On a trip to Puerto Rico, I decided not to buy anything but to "find" my souvenirs: a field trip name tag for "Luis" with a looped sky-blue ribbon, a bird feather, a napkin in neon colors. At home I file the remaining sheets and objects in a large plastic box for referral or memory tracking as hard proof of soft travel.

The hard proofs are what sink me, clutter my fantasized minimal lifestyle, and supply documentation of not fully wrapped nostalgia. With shelves of photograph albums (each trip received a full album in earlier years), the many scrawled travel journals and now the plastic boxes, I am often overwhelmed by my travel collection. Digitization will happen, because I see no other answer, but then do I rip the photos in half and burn, scrutinize each Memory Card, or begin to weed the iPhone images? Last year my books began to overwhelm me in a comparable way. The 800 or so in my dining room, all sitting contently in floor- to-ceiling IKEA bookcases (in my retired librarian arrangement of the month) began to appear yellow and harbor more dust than a Swiffer could remove. The annoyance was slight at first—no disintegration of bindings, but then the vole died behind the piano leaving blackened marks beneath it, and the wood floors had to be resurfaced leading to a desperate four step plan: scrutinize titles, move books, keep only five years of travel books (same as public libraries) and find placement for three-quarters of the collection.

I bled terribly after the first "paper cut" and entered a full five stage grief process running my finger over the edge of faded pages and searching for verbs I would never see again, but I love my minimal bookcases and what remains of everyday books, of travel.

I have abandoned hiking shoes in Peru; shorts and tops somewhere in the Caribbean; jeans in Russia because of little suitcase room—and because I convinced myself that the need was great in those areas for clothing donations. (Each item is designated for a specific person; I do not dump in hotel rooms.) The space I gain back from these donations is mind-altering and peaceful. What I may be attempting is to reach that pinnacle where I return one day with the clothes on my back, a passport and an empty suitcase. No things. The stories of item disposal fill my need.

But there is always that one last object, that non-accessory, pleading for admission to the collection.

Seven years ago, I visited Santiago, Cuba and found a small mystery (misterio) wooden box with a replica of Cuban flag on its surface. Side note: I collect tiny boxes. The box dimension was 5"x 3"x 1", and I wanted it, but I felt I had to rationalize the need, the space.

The box seller, with a face eclipsed by a toothy grin, held the box between thumb and forefinger finger in both hands, pulled one hand away and made a Houdini circle in the air with his free hand in a very enticing fashion. Then with two fingers he opened the box, shut it, and handed it to me.

"Cinco dolares."

How did he open it? I struggled with the triangles on its side. "Abrir?" I think of the shell game played by vendors on New York City sidewalks.

His impossible grin broadened, and he shook his head. "Cinco dolares primero."

I handed him the money while figuring out that I would create a space for the box, because the story and object merited that action. One more large grin and he trotted off to entice another tourist and leaving me without the secret to the opening.

The box created discussion with visitors to my house—and frustration. No one could figure out how to open the thing—until a friend happened across a YouTube video of the exact box (not a hand-crafted item apparently) two months later and opened it in seconds.

The box now sits in the center of my mantel with my full consent.

What the Dickens?
Lisa Williams

Glen was surprised to find a complete set of Folio Dickens novels in his local charity shop.

He had the same set at home, they were the pride of his collection; he felt pleased that, like he did, they'd displayed them in order of publication, not alphabetically. His finger lingered on a spine and he looked forward to returning to his own books.

When he got back, he was met by a gaping space on his carefully organised shelves. He shouted to his wife wondering if she could shed some light on the situation, but it seemed she'd gone too.

The Cost of Our Baggage
Sarah-Jane Gill

Dense, threatening, charcoal-coloured clouds hung low in the sky. There were no shadows with no light to cast them. Beth could hear a river flowing, fast and roaring, but she couldn't see the water. She could see a queue, a square brown building and beyond it a boat. A tall masted dark wood structure that didn't bob or lilt despite the roar of the water it must have been sitting in.

The person in front of her shuffled forward. Beth automatically followed suit. She realised she had no idea how she got there, no idea what they were queueing for. A single file line. People of all ages, shapes, shades of skin tone, national dress. Some were waiting calmly, gazing up at the blackened sky. Some fidgeted nervously, darting panicked looks around them. One she saw sobbing softly into a handkerchief. Nobody spoke. Nobody looked at each other. They faced forwards and shuffled, shuffled and shuffled again towards the plain brown building.

Beth reached the front of the queue eventually and a door opened for her. She stepped through it and found she was the only person from the queue inside, even though she had seen so many pass through doors before her. It was a large room with a single empty desk, a hard looking chair on one side and a figure on the other. Clothed in the same colours as the wall, somehow with features as plain as the desk itself, the person was so indistinct that Beth struggled to retain any information about them at all, even with them sitting right in front of her. A hand gestured to the chair and she sat down.

'You cannot pass until your baggage is checked.'

Beth looked down at her side and found her hand wrapped around the hard handle of an old suitcase. She pulled gently at it, it was heavy, almost crushingly heavy. How had she not felt it before? A cold fear settled in her stomach, she had no idea why but was certain it was valid. Like waking from a terrible dream and carrying the certain dread with you into the waking world when the cause had been left firmly in the subconscious.

'You cannot pass until your baggage is checked.'

'What happens if I can't pass?' she asked.

The figure nodded towards the wall beside them. The surface appeared fogged then cleared to reveal some sort of window. Through that window Beth saw a waiting room. It was crowded with people hunched over baggage, eyes deeply lost and haunted, stuck.

'You cannot pass until your baggage is checked.'

Beth swallowed hard. She used both hands to haul the suitcase clumsily up onto the desk. She recognised this case from her childhood. It was an old fashioned boxy rectangular case, fake leather sort of covering, with brass style snaps keeping it shut. It's usual storage place had been underneath her Grandmother's bed. Partially obscured by bedsheets covered in little purple flowers and shrouded by the smell of talcum powder. She had never seen it open. She clicked on the clasps and they flipped back, slowly she lifted the lid until it was fully open for them both to see.

It was full of orbs. Deep with swirling colours, each different from the next. The looked like galaxy systems or storm clouds. So many sizes as well, some like marbles, some tennis ball sized and two that seemed enormous, the size of a head.

'What are they?' she heard herself stammer.

'Secrets.'

She reached out to touch one, brushed her fingers gently against what felt like the finest possible glass. The memory slammed into her mind, five year old hands tucking screwed up foil wrappers under a mattress and furiously rubbing chocolate from her mouth. She wrenched her hand back in shock, so vivid, too vivid. The figure watched her, not to the orbs.

'I thought you needed to check this. What are you checking?'

The figure continued to watch her with no expression. She found herself reaching out again, memories flooding her mind. Things she took that she wasn't supposed to, untruths she used to smooth a gritty path, rules unfollowed, gentle gestures kept to the confines of her own heart to save the ego of others. Then one of the larger ones.

She bolted back in her chair. Her mind screamed at her, the memory she had shut out for so long. The birth certificate, the name in soft swirling writing, the flames swallowing it up forever. She wrenched herself back, nausea rising up into her chest. She blinked hard. Still the figure was watching her.

'And the other.'

Nausea threatened to bubble over but she reached for the other orb. Again her mind screamed. The door closing in front of the desperate eyes looking out at her, begging her to do something, anything to make it stop. But she didn't. Because she knew those eyes would belong to her if she did. Bile spilled out onto the floor below her, leaving acidic yellow trails on her clothes. It sank into the ground and dissolved without a trace.

'These secrets weigh too much. You cannot carry them with you.' The figure said firmly.

'But what can I do?'

'You must release them back to the living.'

Release them back to the living. Beth felt a cold chill settle in her bones. They would know, they would know she kept these things from her, that she was nothing more than a selfish, vicious, vapid being. They would misunderstand, they wouldn't know how scared she was, what the consequences were, it was a different time, they would never understand. All the things she had tried to protect, love, respect, would be lost. It was to protect them, to keep them safe. They would hate her. And she would not be able to do anything to control it.

'You can opt not to travel on.'

The window cleared again beside them and Beth understood now the haunting of the eyes, the weight of the baggage at their feet or clutched into their arms. She felt a tear slide down her cheek, hot and unrelenting.

'You must make your choice. Others are waiting.'

Slowly she picked up the orb. Disgust ran through every nerve in her body, she held it out, closing her eyes tightly against the visions flooding her mind. Instinct trapping her with them. The figure took it and Beth gasped as her body and mind were instantly cleansed. Like glacier water soothing every vein and nerve. She reached for the other, shame flooding and then cleansing. Then another, milder, smaller, but full of self-hate, then cleansing. And again and again until there were only little marbles left at the bottom of the case.

'That's enough.' The figure said as she was mid reach.

Relief and exhaustion made her arms so heavy they sank past her lap and dangled over the sides of her chair. She felt numb, empty, and shocked. A door opened behind the figure and a hand was held up to direct her towards it. The figure gently closed the case and clicked the clasps down. Beth had no idea where the orbs she had handed over had gone but there was no trace of them in the room. She stood, joints shaking and picked up the case. It was so light she could barely feel it in her hands.

Wordlessly she went through the door and felt a soft waft of air behind her as it closed. She was on the dock side now. A less organised queue of people were walking over to the boat she had seen before. It was huge, dark, tethered to hooks on the shore by massive ropes. There was a steep gangway that had been obscured by the brown building, at the base of it stood Death. Tall, hooded, nodding gently as the passengers passed one by one. She found herself walking past, accepting comfort in the gentle shepherding away from the shore.

There was a seat, in a large galley, she sank into it clutched onto her bag. Eventually she felt the soft lilt of the boat move, sink away from the dock and into the free running river. Gentle rolling soothed her like a baby being rocked in warm loving arms. As they moved away from the shore she felt the slow release, the separating of atoms and particles, until finally she dissipated completely into freedom. The case left alone under an empty seat.

The Remove
David H Weinberger

Henry noticed the hands thrown up in apparent helplessness, the shoulders shrug in frustration, saw the lips form the words, 'redundant,' 'reorganization,' 'hard times,' though they seemed to float in a misty cloud with no apparent connection to himself. Still, through it all, Henry deciphered the message that he was being fired. Feeling present but set apart from the action, somehow not related to him, was reminiscent of the peacefulness he felt as a child playing in the dirt with his Ginocars, his self-imposed bubble protecting him, and his surroundings becoming indistinct. Back then he had easily slid into the distance between himself and a world which frightened him, one he did not understand, one in which he felt he did not belong.

The young Henry had commandeered a small spot of dirt nestled at the edge of his father's rhododendron garden. He pulled weeds and cleared rocks, used them to demarcate the boundaries of his invented city. He checked that the two treads were still working on the orange bulldozer, his most prized Ginocar. Satisfied, he pushed it around the dirt patch, building roads for the rest of his collection lined up at the edge. As his invented city took shape, Henry felt the turmoil inside settle down. He sank into the feeling of soil grinding into his legs, the honey-like scent of nearby plants, the blur of passing vehicles, and the vibration in his hands as he pushed the Ginocars across the dirt.

"Are you even listening to me?" his soon to be ex-boss asked.

"Listening, but not understanding," Henry replied.

"What is it you're not understanding?"

"How to recapture the part of me I lost along with my Ginocars."

"I don't know what that means, Henry. But, good luck to you."

In an effort to be conciliatory, an enduring but not always self-promoting trait, Henry thanked his boss, shook hands, and left the office. He felt no malice or disappointment because he never really thought the job was right for him. A stroke of luck landed him the position and he knew it was a matter of time before people saw through his charade. Besides, his sudden recollection crowded out any remorse he may have mustered on this auspicious day, containing as it did a certain curative.

Ted, the security guard assigned to escort Henry out of the building, coaxed him to fill his box and head to the exit.

"Ted?" Henry said as he cleared his desk. "Did you ever collect Ginocars?"

"Nah. Hot Wheels. Loved the redlines."

"Yeah, those were cool. I only had Ginocars."

Collecting Ginocars instead of the more desired diecasts started when Henry was a toddler. His parents could not afford the pricier Matchboxes, and certainly not the gleaming Hot Wheels which Henry eyed every Saturday when they walked through Kmart. He was fated to collect the cheaper Ginocars. They were bulky and weirdly out of sync with reality: wheels a bit too large, no headlights or windows, and unrealistic colors, more in keeping with cheap plastic toys found in bubblegum dispensers than on actual cars.

Henry didn't abandon his dream of owning the better toy cars but he was sufficiently content with his collection and each new vehicle his parents gifted him, and the cars would prove helpful in his future remove. He spent several years escaping with his Ginocars to the dirt patch. While he had other interests, like books, puzzles, and movies, none of them offered the same serenity. He was often tempted to pursue a friendship with a new neighbor, or explore a different part of the neighborhood on his bike, but he could never bring himself to do so, afraid of being rejected or believing that he was too weak to survive outside the bubble he had created and maintained. The unknown entities in the world were more powerful than his motivation to reach out.

"Bad luck for you," Ted replied. "Much like today."

Ted followed Henry to the front door and held it open as Henry exited. They nodded to one another in passing, the most either could muster to acknowledge what they both saw as a tenuous and forced relationship.

Once he made it to the street, Henry deposited his box of worthless, personal belongings he had accumulated the past four years next to the first garbage can he encountered. The pens and pencils, motivational calendar from two years back, drink coasters, and useless paperweights blended in seamlessly with the overflowing trash. The only keepsake he held onto was the pale blue AMC Jeep Ginocar he had pulled from his mom's trashing years ago when he had turned twelve. At that late stage, while most children had developed peer groups and were likely experimenting with sex and drugs, he was still playing with his Ginocars in the dirt patch, albeit without the same joy, without the same level of comfort as when he was younger. And his mother, worried that his infatuation with his cars would be another source of ridicule from his peers, inadvertently upended the little comfort he had carved out.

"You're nearly a teenager," his mother told him. "Don't you think you're a bit old to be playing with little cars?"

"Those are my favorite things, mom."

"What about your books? Those are better, aren't they?"

"The books are great. But I feel better outside with my Ginocars."

"But most of them are broken. It's been a long time since we gave you any new ones. Your dad and I thought you would have outgrown them by now."

"They're fine the way they are. I don't know what I'd do without them."

"I'm sorry, Henry," his mother continued, "but it's for the best."

The discussion ended with his mom dumping the Ginocars in the trash and Henry's life in the dirt patch, his fragile grip on comfort, came to an end.

With his job and all evidence of it gone, Henry felt free to pursue anything he desired the rest of the day. The wise thing, he thought, would be to go home and update his resume. Alternatively, he could do that tomorrow and waste the rest of the day sitting on a bench or drinking at the pub. But overriding each idea was the growing sense that he should use his newfound time to replace his old Ginocars. It was a thought whose infancy only surfaced as he sat across from his boss. In the short time since his firing it had morphed into a calling, a purpose, a quest with a holy grail at its conclusion.

Henry did an internet search on his phone and laughed at the meager three results. He clicked the first hit and was surprised by its brevity. 'Ginocars, the failed die cast manufacturer,' the text read, 'had a brief production run starting in 1970, issuing 27 different 1/64 scale cars and trucks. The company declared bankruptcy in 1973 due to infamously poor quality.'

Henry remembered the poor quality. Many times, a pebble would lodge in the hollow of a wheel, hit up against the chassis, and prevent the wheels from turning. He would force a pudgy finger into the crevasse to dislodge it and inevitably bend the fragile axle or pop the wheel off, relegating that particular toy to the parts pail. Sometimes, the body would separate from the chassis and snap the tabs holding them together, rendering the toy completely useless. Of course, Henry blamed himself for the breakage, believing he simply lacked the knowledge or dexterity to properly care for his collection. It never occurred to him that the toys were deficient from the beginning and responsible for their own demise.

Henry did a second search for local used die cast toys, thinking there must be several antique stores where he could find piles of Ginocars. He got plenty of results and chose Casting Call, the closest store selling collectible used toys.

"Where are the Ginocars?" Henry asked after failing to see any stocked on a dizzying array of shelves. "You've got Matchbox, Hot Wheels, Corgi, even Happy Meal cars. I don't see any Ginocars."

"Not a one," the shop owner said. "The wheels and axles were always breaking. Like, a stone would get lodged…"

"I know the story, please spare me. You must have some broken ones? Maybe in the back?"

"Sorry. Pretty much useless stuff. A bit fragile compared to Matchbox and Hot Wheels. I have lots of those in packages if you'd like."

"No, it has to be Ginocars."

"Sorry. If you really need those, and I can't imagine why you would, you could contact Gino himself. He might be able to help you."

"What do you mean, Gino? That's a person?"

"Of course, Gino Gastiricci. Started the company early seventies. Lost a lot of money, but he's still around. In his eighties or so. Somewhere north of the city. Look him up."

After extensive searching, Henry found an address for Gino Gastiricci, living in a remote town outside the city. While driving to the location, Henry anticipated the museum-like aura of the Ginocar birthplace, maybe with commemorative plaques, neon signs, a long line to get in to see the displays. But as he pulled up to the basic suburban home he wondered if he had arrived at the correct address, if he had been misled into believing this was the home of the Ginocar creator. He hesitated a moment before approaching the house, worried he would be incapable of following through and knocking on the door. But he dug deep for courage believing he was steps away from his treasure trove, and gently knocked.

"Mr. Gastiricci?" Henry began once the door was opened by a slightly bent man.

"Yes, but call me Gino."

"Gino. My name is Henry and I understand you are the man behind Ginocars."

"Wow, Ginocars. Haven't heard that name in a long time."

"Yeah, me either. Just popped into my head this morning. As well as really good memories of playing with those cars. I was wondering if you have any I could purchase from you."

"Purchase? Son, those things stopped selling a long time ago."

"I know. I was hoping you might have some left over."

"I have a bunch but they may not be what you're expecting. I'll tell you what. Let me finish my coffee and then I'll show you the cars."

Gino took Henry to the kitchen and poured him a coffee.

"If you don't mind my asking, why are you looking for Ginocars?" Gino asked between sips of coffee.

"I don't exactly know, but as my boss was firing me this morning, I started thinking about this busted car I had sitting on my desk." Henry showed Gino the Jeep. Gino smiled, took it from Henry, and spun it in his hands.

"Oh, Henry, this was a good one. I can't believe you still have it."

"I snuck it from the trash after my mom threw out my entire collection. I had a bunch and I used to play with them in a dirt patch near the garden. I started thinking about the ones my mom trashed and the joy I had as a kid playing with Ginocars."

"You sure it was joy you recollect?" Gino asked.

Henry had to admit, he wasn't sure it was joy so much as an absence of pain, a closing off of the world around him, one he preferred not to engage with. Hard to believe it was thirty years ago, when he was six and just starting school, that he came face-to-face with a previously unknown darkness during recess at Edgar Elementary School. His kindergarten class had finished story time and Henry was buzzing with excitement from the teacher's reading of how a princess had outsmarted a dragon to save a prince. He ran with his classmates out the door with no particular goal in mind, other than to bask in the next surprise awaiting him. He slowed down and it seemed impossibly perfect that this bounty would be available to him every day: storytelling, monkey bars, swings, basketball hoops. And laughing, running kids everywhere.

"What the hell are you looking at?" an older boy asked. Henry wasn't looking at the boy so he was unaware that the question was aimed at him. He didn't answer, walked on. The boy, unaccustomed to being ignored, followed him.

"Hey, dickhead! Answer me when I talk to you!" And then the inevitable schoolyard bullying session commenced where a superior-feeling individual exorcizes his demons by trampling a smaller, gentler being. The boy pushed Henry to the ground, sat on his chest, spit in his face, and explained how he ruled the playground and let Henry know that in the future he didn't want to see him anywhere near him. The boy left Henry sniveling in the dirt wearing an invisible badge labeling him as a loser, an easy target, and as an eternal recipient of anybody's wrath.

From that moment on, Henry internalized everything thrown at him. The name-calling, the taunts, the beatings, coalesced into a force powerful enough to make Henry question what he knew of himself. He took this force to be more knowledgeable, better able to identify who he really was. Over a very short time, he abandoned his previously held beliefs about himself, that he was kind, intelligent, likable. And unable to offer a counterargument to his abusers, or even a defense, he put his energy into closing himself off. To building a wall to hide behind. Henry didn't share his school ordeals with his parents or siblings. He kept it inside where it rumbled and made his body feel like it was ready to explode. It was painful in the beginning but with time Henry acclimated to the discomfort and came to believe it was how everyone felt. So maybe it wasn't exactly joy he felt playing with Ginocars but it was the nearest he could find.

"Henry?" Gino pushed.

"Yeah, I'm sure. Loads of joy playing with your cars for hours every day."

"Alone?"

"Just me and my Ginocars."

"They ever break?"

"All the time."

"Didn't that bother you?"

"Sure. But it's what I had and I can't explain the calm I experienced sitting in the dirt alone, with my Ginocars. It was like the Earth stopped spinning, like nothing and no one could touch me. Like things were going to be okay."

"And were they?"

"They were for a while. But then it started to fade. Just like today. Anyway, I had this crazy idea I could rebuild that imaginary dirt city, populate it with Ginocars, and recapture that calm."

"Sorry to say, it does sound a little crazy. But, I think I can help. Come on."

Henry followed Gino into a small bedroom, now used as storage for thousands of die casts. Henry froze, staring at the cars stretching from floor to ceiling, on tables and cabinets throughout the room.

"I know what you're thinking," Gino said. "Here is the enemy. Right?"

"Exactly," Henry replied. "These should be Ginocars."

"I never made even close to this many. These models are what I wanted to create. They were successful, well-made, and kids wanted them. Adults wanted them! Ginocars were never that good. They couldn't compete with these, and they were poorly made. The cars and the company were basically failures."

"But I loved those cars," Henry interjected. "They were not failures."

"Your love doesn't change the fact the enterprise failed. Cars broke. They fell apart as kids pushed them around, lasted no longer than a week, maybe two. Lost tons of money. Finally shut down the whole operation. Three years. That's all."

"I played with them for twice that long."

Gino laughed. "If only more customers had been that tolerant. Thanks for that Henry."

"You're welcome. So, I'm dying here! Where are they?" Gino shushed him with his raised hands. He opened a closet door, stood aside, and invited Henry to look inside.

"This is what's left of my efforts," Gino said.

The closet had a small shelf unit stacked with a few cardboard boxes and colorful beach pails. Henry saw hundreds of Ginocars piled in the pails and wondered with excitement what was in the boxes. As expected, he felt an immediate release of tension, the feeling of looking through the wrong end of a telescope, a laser-focused view of the Ginocars. Just like when he was in the dirt patch.

"There's a bit left over from production," Gino explained, "but not much. I was smart enough to stop building before I was left holding inventory. Most of this is trash. Broken cars kids and parents sent back to me, or stores returned to me. But this one," Gino said, pulling a sealed package from one of the boxes, "I'm very proud of. Here, you can have it."

The box had a picture of an orange bulldozer printed on it. Henry gently shook the box and heard the tiny sound of a die cast hitting the sides.

"My God! Is there really one in there?"

"There is."

"That's fantastic! How much do you want for it?"

"It's a gift to a fan. Take this too," Gino said, handing Henry a pail of broken Ginocars. "But consider before you delve too deep into this pail. You might be better off leaving it behind. I was once like you, isolating myself from things around me. Occasionally reaching out from my little bubble to get a piece of the world but missing it by a fraction. Hell, maybe by a mile. Either way, it kept on spinning without me. Left me with nothing but broken Ginocars and a lot of solitude. You need to get out there Henry. It's there for you as much as for the next guy."

"I sort of like the solitude, though," Henry replied, clutching the pail of cars to his chest.

"Ok, Henry. Whatever you say. But listen, I have to go now. It was a pleasure meeting you and I hope things work out for you."

Henry found himself alone on the front porch with Gino's words echoing in his head. He knew the childhood dirt patch provided a remove from the things that threatened him when he was younger, things that created a sadness larger than him. And he knew he never really left the dirt patch. In some fashion, he had always isolated himself with some sort of remove: books, wine, solitary walks. But looking back on what he removed himself from, considering what he may have missed because of it, the very little that people actually had to offer, the endless attacks and general ill will of others, he thought the remove might not be a bad thing.

Henry found a nearby park and sat under a pine tree, just off the paved path, sending small puffs of dust into the air. He looked to see if others were observing a grown man sitting in the dirt, but nobody seemed to pay him any mind, no different from his peers that passed him as he played in the dirt patch as a child. Henry swept his hand through dirt and pine needles, careful to remove any trouble-making pebbles.

He unwrapped the bulldozer and gently turned the treads with a finger, happy to see them function properly. He pushed it through the dirt and began a new town for the Ginocars waiting in the pail. Once he had a main road, side streets, homes and apartments, and a few parking lots, Henry set the bulldozer aside and then put the pale blue Jeep on one of the roads. He rummaged through the pail and discovered a Plymouth Duster, a Chevrolet Vega, an AMC Gremlin, a lime green El Camino. They were scratched and battered, missing several pieces, and reminiscent of his childhood collection. Henry sifted dirt through his hands, breathed in the pine scent surrounding him, and poured out the rest of the Ginocars. Everything else was a blur.

Stella
Sara Wilson

She has become this fur coat
tossed at the end of the night
onto its hook, shoulders turned blades;
thin hips, like tines.
Her ribs bellow with the breeze
from the closing door.

How small can a cat shrink?
Her meows become the sound of lips parting,
teeth, tombstones beneath a tongue.
How much longer will the ghosts of the wrens
and pine warblers keep driving
these hungry bones into my hand?

Out of my League
Katie Kent

"I haven't seen you here before." The woman at the bar flicks her blonde hair back, sipping nonchalantly from a margarita glass rimmed with salt. She's probably early 30s, like me, but has an air of confidence about her that I can only dream of possessing.

My stomach flips, and I open and close my mouth like a goldfish, then settle for a lame, "Hi."

A smile flickers across her face. "What's your name?"

"J… Joey," I stutter.

"Joey," she repeats, giving my name a sultry edge. "Can I buy you a drink?"

I just gawp at her. This woman is so far out of my league we may as well be in different cities. Maybe she's trying to pull a practical joke on me. Or her friends have dared her to ask me out. If I say yes, maybe she'll burst into laughter and tell me she's not gay. She's got long eyelashes and grips her glass with elegant fingers, the nails painted a bright shade of red.

*

"Mum?" I yelled, opening the fridge and pulling out a can of Coke. "Are you home?" I was 13 and I'd just got home from school.

The silence I was met with suggested not, but when I climbed the stairs, I heard a noise from her room.

"Mum?" Still no response. Pressing my ear to her closed door, I jumped back when I heard a sob. My heart racing, I pressed the door handle down and pushed the door open.

Mum was sat on the bed, her eyes red, tears streaming down her cheeks.

"What's happened?" I rushed over to her side immediately.

She gave a weak smile through the tears. "Sorry, Joey. I'm just feeling a bit sad at the moment. It's nothing to worry about."

I'd never seen Mum cry before. "Is it Dad?" I asked, my heart pounding. "Has something happened to him?"

She flinched. "Your dad is fine." There was a bitterness to her voice. "He's just… we're going to take a little time apart."

"What? Why?"

Then she said the words I would remember for the rest of my life. "He's found someone he likes better than me."

*

"Drink?" the woman prompts again, pulling me out of my daze. I scan her face for any signs of dishonesty, but she's so gorgeous that all I can focus on are her sharp cheekbones highlighted with a pale pink blusher, the way her bright blue eyes rimmed with a smoky grey eyeshadow bore into mine, and how her full lips would feel pressed against mine.

I cough. "I'd better be getting back to my friends."

Is that disappointment I see cross her face? "Suit yourself." She shrugs as I walk back to my table, holding a bottle of beer by the neck and a glass of gin and tonic in one hand, and a glass of white wine in the other.

"What did the woman at the bar want?" Sadie asks, as I sit down at the table, sliding the beer bottle towards her.

I feel my face go bright red. "Nothing."

Nina scrutinizes my face. "Josephine Rachel Anderson, was she chatting you up?"

I bite my thumbnail, looking down at the table. "She offered to buy me a drink. But it was probably just a joke."

"Why would it be a joke?"

I look back over to the bar. The woman is looking straight at me. She waves, and I quickly drop my gaze again. "Just look at her."

"She's gorgeous," Nina says. "And?"

"As if someone like that would be interested in someone like me."

Sadie sighs. "Mate, how many times have we been through this? Why wouldn't she be interested in you?"

"I'm hardly a catch." I've always hated the way my ears stick out, the fact that I have to wear glasses, my flat chest.

"She can't take her eyes off you," Sadie points out.

"She's probably looking at you."

Sadie rolls her eyes. "Sure she is. So she chats you up at the bar and then makes eyes at one of your friends?"

I just shrug. "Even if she is looking at me, she'll soon lose interest."

*

"Helen is pregnant. I'm going to have a son."

I stared at Dad in shock. Him shacking up with another woman was one thing, but a baby? I had just turned 15; surely he was too old to be looking after a newborn.

He thrust a photo at me. "Here's the scan. Look at his legs! He'll be a strong one for sure."

Mum came in with a cup of tea, which she put down on the coffee table in front of Dad.

"Did you know about this?" I asked her. "Did you know they're having a baby?"

"Yes." She smiles at me, but it's strained. "It's great news."

"You'll have a little half-brother." Dad beamed. "Isn't that exciting?"

I just glared at him. How could I tell him I felt like I was being replaced?

*

Sadie and Nina exchange glances.

"Don't do that," I say. "Don't look at me like I'm the most annoying woman on the planet."

"Joey, the only one who thinks you are the most annoying woman on the planet is you." Nina sips her wine. "We just frustrated, that's all. You have so much to offer a woman. We just wish you could see it."

I stir my gin and tonic with my straw. "You have to say that. You're my friends."

"Oh my God." Sadie puts her head in her hands. "Why do you think we're your friends? It's because we like you. You're a likeable person. But you need more confidence and self-esteem."

"I can't help the way I feel." I hear the defensive tone to my voice.

"You know what our response to that is." Nina fixes her eyes upon my face, and I feel myself wilt.

"I've told you before, I'm not going to counselling."

Sadie looks up. "Then go and ask her out, already."

"I can't."

She shakes her head. "Want me to ask her out for you?"

"Just drop it. She's not even my type," I lie.

"Sure she's not. Hey, don't look now." Nina nudges me with her hip. "She's on her way over."

"What?" I swallow, looking over- and sure enough, the woman is walking towards us. Now she's standing, I can see her bright blue dress has a slit right down one leg, showing off a pair of perfectly-toned, long legs, which does nothing to temper down the lust I'm feeling.

"Pick your jaw off the floor," Nina whispers in my ear, and I feel myself blush.

When the woman gets to our table, she hands me a piece of paper.

"What's this?" I ask, taking it from her outstretched fingers.

"My phone number. Look, I think you're cute. When you've stopped playing hard to get, give me a call." She turns and walks away from our table, then out of the bar, not looking back.

*

"Have you heard from Dad?"

Mum can't look me in the eye, fixing her gaze upon a point above my head. "I'm really sorry, Joey. He won't be able to make it."

I chew my lip. "Let me guess, Ant has a football match or something?"

"Sports Day at school." Mum gives me a sympathetic smile. "I'm sorry."

"It's not your fault." I blink the tears away from my eyes. "I should have known he wouldn't come."

"I hate the way he treats you."

I shrug. "It's fine."

"It's not fine." She puts her hand on my arm. "Joey, this is your university graduation! Your dad ought to be here. I hate that he always puts him first. I know you struggle with it."

"Can we change the subject?" I plead. I don't want to cry at my graduation ceremony. I shouldn't care. Dad has shown again and again how little I mean to him.

*

"Have you called her yet?" Sadie asks, at lunchtime at work on Monday. "Please tell me you two 'hung out' all weekend." She does air quotes with her fingers.

"Don't be silly. I barely even thought about her."

"Sure you didn't." Nina can't keep the smirk off her face, and I feel my face get hot.

I rub my eyes. Can she tell I stayed up late last night checking out Krysta's Instagram profile? That I almost texted her, so many times, but chickened out at the last minute?

"I don't know why you keep bringing this up."

"We're just trying to help you," Sadie says. "I mean, when was the last time you had sex?"

I almost choke on my coffee. "That's none of your business."

"Years?" she guesses. My silence shows her she's hit the nail on the head. "Don't you miss it?"

"I don't need sex." I fold my arms defensively.

"Everyone needs sex. In the bar, you were staring at Krystal like you wanted to rip her clothes off then and there."

I feel my cheeks heat up. "Don't be stupid," I mumble. "I don't need her. She's just a woman."

"A super-hot woman, who gave you her phone number." Nina sighs. "Honestly, how much more encouragement do you need? If it was me, I'd be engaged to her already."

I shake my head. "You call her, if you like her that much."

"And you'd be happy for me to date her, would you?"

I chew on my lip. Would I be happy if Krystal started dating one of my friends? I sigh. "Look, I want to call her. But I'm scared. What if she thinks I'm boring? What if she dumps me after one date? What if I get my hopes up only to have my heart broken?"

*

"It's Louise. We think you're too good for her," Allie said.

"We've been over this. I love her. I know you guys don't like her, but she's my soulmate. I'd appreciate it if you didn't bring this up again."

"Joey, she's cheating on you," Ben blurted out.

"What?!" I felt the colour drain from my face. "Why would you say something like that?"

Allie put her hand on my arm. "It's true. I saw her at a club the other night, her tongue down some guy's throat."

I felt like I was going to be sick. "Maybe you were mistaken. Maybe it was just someone that looked like her."

Allie shook her head. "It was her, J. I'd recognise that arrogant swagger anywhere. Plus I saw her face. I'm sorry."

"What night?"

"Saturday."

Louise had told me she was going to a friend's house on Saturday night. Tears pricked at the corners of my eyes. "I knew it was too good to be true. To think that someone like her could be into someone like me."

"Mate, this isn't your fault." But it was always my fault.

*

"Don't do this to yourself." Sadie's eyes are full of pity. "We get that you've been hurt in the past, but not everyone is like Louise."

"Or your dad," Nina adds, softly.

I only realise I'm crying when my vision starts to blur.

"Oh, Joey." Sadie rubs my back with her hand. "Look, we can't promise you that this will end well. But what if it does? What if she's the one? Sometimes you have to take a risk, for a chance at happiness."

"I can't go through all that again." I look down at the remnants of my lunch on the table. "What if she's only interested in sex? What if she's seeing other people? What if we want different things?"

"You need to stop with the 'what ifs'." Nina smiles at me. "The only way you'll know what her intentions are are to ask her."

Pins and needles are spreading through my legs. "I can't call a woman and ask her if she just wants sex or a long-term relationship. She'll think I'm nuts."

"No, that would be silly," Nina agrees, spearing a piece of pasta with her fork. "But you could call her, arrange a date, and then suss out her intentions, subtly, on the date. At the very least, you could get a decent snog out of her."

I feel my cheeks heat up. "But what if-."

"Uh-uh. No more 'what ifs'. Just call her."

*

"Hey, babe. Fancy a quickie?" Louise grabbed my hand and pulled me towards her. My lips inches from hers, I struggled to focus. She was the hottest woman I'd ever met. I couldn't believe it when she'd asked me out. Maybe the others were wrong about what they saw?

I took a deep breath, my legs shaking. "Have you been cheating on me?"

She laughed. "What?" She took a lock of my hair, winding it around her finger. Her perfume filled my nostrils. The smell was unfamiliar, and there was a sinking feeling in my stomach.

"Whose perfume is that?" I blurted out. "And don't lie to me."

She let go of my hair and took a step back. "Oh, Joey." There was a smirk on her face. "Did you really think you were enough for me?"

My eyes filled with tears, and she rolled her eyes. "Look, you're a good shag, that's for sure. But you're soooooooooo boring. All you want to do is stay in and watch TV."

"How many?" I blinked back the tears. How could I have missed the signs?

"It's not like I've been counting."

"Get out." My voice was calmer than I felt. "Get out of my house. I never want to see you again."

"Whatever." Her tone was disinterested, and I wondered how long I'd been ignoring the signs for. "I have a queue of women and men who are just begging to date me."

"GET OUT!"

*

"Hello?"

Krysta's voice does funny things to my insides.

"H… hey." My voice is croaky. "It's Joey. We met in the bar the other night. You gave me your number. I mean… it was Saturday night. About 9pm."

She laughs gently. "I remember you, Joey. It's not like I give my number out to women all the time, you know."

I start to relax. "You don't?"

"I don't. There was something about you. I'm glad you called."

I feel a smile break out on my face. "Me too."

There's a brief silence, then she prompts, "So? Why **did** you call?"

"Oh, yeah, sorry." I giggle, feeling like a kid talking to their first crush. "Well, I, uh… I wondered if you wanted to, you know…"

She laughs. "Are you trying to ask me out, Joey?"

I twirl my hair around my finger. "Yes."

"The answer's yes."

*

I've tried on five different outfits, dismissing each one for some reason or another. This skirt is too short. This one makes my boobs look too small. This one makes them look too big. Yellow looks awful against my pale skin. This one makes me look like a frumpy, middle-aged woman.

Pulling the last dress off, I sigh, lying back on my bed in just my underwear. What am I doing? She's so beautiful, and I'm so ordinary. There's no way this will last. I'm just setting myself up for disappointment.

My phone pings, and I pull myself back to my feet, walking over to my chest of drawers and picking the phone up.

'Can't wait to see you x'.

Dread floods through my body, making me double over. She'll get bored of me. I'll only let her down. She deserves much better than me.

Calmly, I delete her messages, go into my contacts and delete her number, then prepare myself for another Saturday night in front of the TV.

Sleeping
Devon Neal

Tonight the moon laces
through the blind gaps
brighter than last night,
and in the lunar blue
collecting in our unlit
bedroom, I see your
face, shuttered and
sighing, asleep near my
shoulder. Your hand cradles
your face, your elbow
folded, the bedsheet
collared against your
chin. Moonlight collects
in a pool in the valley
of your waist, below
the slope of your hips.
Your bare feet bloom
from the blanket,
outstretched, ankle
bones ghostly under
the moon's broken face.
I can almost feel
faint forearm hairs
brushing against my skin.
Tomorrow, when day
finds a name, left here is
a blanket like a windswept
leaf, bedsheets wrinkle-
bitten and clean, smelling
only of me.

You Step Into Your Therapist's Office
Alley Shubert

he's sitting on the floor surrounded by his scattered lunch
papers in disarray and vitamins thrown about
he tells you he's sorry but suddenly he feels like he is
seven years old again corned in the fetal position and the
trauma comes crashing down on him
like a ton of bricks

you can lay on the couch or stretch out near salt lamps or
pretend to meditate during a sound bath or
practice TRE on the floor and all of the EMDR
your tiny hummingbird heart desires but buried deep down
way down in the pit of your belly where you spill out the
thick black goo of your guts knowing no matter what you say or do
the trauma will always remain somewhere in the
yellow muscle of your heart

you envision this spiritual journey and
tell your therapist you want to travel alone
to feel the canyon burst through your bones
taste nothing but white sands on your tongue
but fear you are abandoning your son and still
you want to drive a red convertible top down
tell yourself you're beautiful
because sometimes we need to feel like
we come from sunshine and stardust

you thank your therapist for showing you a
first hand account of what it is to be human
how take a step back and know that even
those who are meant to guide us
have to face their own demons

you write poetry no one will ever read

you concede rather than bleed

you're a pessimist but believe in hope

after years and years

you are still learning
how to cope

Drowning Sorrow
Melissa Folini

Tonight I drank 'til
life's focus grew cloudy, my steps unsteady, my gestures slow and exaggerated.
You have your addictions and your secrets,
why can't I?
I thought I'd try some rum to start
tomorrow, maybe wine
or nothing.
Am I really the self-destructive kind?

The Critic Inside Your Home
J. Inkwell

It's safer to believe that trust is a weakness
when your doorstep is muddied
with decades-tall piles of soot.
A calculated destruction
consumes you slowly.
Sheltering your eyes from rejection, pain—
misunderstandings.
Double-locking every door.
Closing every curtain.
Preventing the neighbors from
witnessing that gnawing ache.

Trapped inside a stale atmosphere,
each toxic inhalation
finesses its way into your lungs
until you're sore with self-doubt.
Reminiscing on non-existent memories
to keep you lukewarm inside a frigid home.
Brief glances through the glass;
tempting your famine.
Sweet visions serenading
hymns of what could be.
The soft-focus glimmers
entice you with breadcrumbs of hope.
And still, your loyalty remains
to a self-imposed loneliness
that you have believed
you decidedly deserve
long before you knew
what longing really meant.
Curious visitors,
bewildered by your dismissals,
overstay their welcome
yet never stay long enough.

It's easy to run from
the taste of sweeter things
when you are used to a life
that condemns you for truly living.

if i may,
Hayden Finkelshtain

this little death is hard for me. we're two fifths of the way packed and i haven't done my fair share and i'll tell you why. because just like how i'd find those house centipedes with their angular limbs and long bodies hiding in the shadows behind our cutting boards in the corner of the kitchen, and they'd scurry, and i'd capture them in tupperware and release them outside (where it always seemed they'd somehow sneak back in through an unfound crevice, or they had babies before we released them, or something), and i'd shriek 'jesus, fuck' every time. i fear, in that way, that i may come upon some moment, in the shadows, that i cannot pack into a box. i have already found the baths you ran me when i couldn't make sense of things, and cheesecake factory dishes that went cold because we both had new rings on. and i found the time we slept backwards on the mattress because you were upset and i joked that we could 'try a new perspective'. i found a lot. more than just those. but i've already spent a few weeks dealing with my accidental rediscoveries. compartmentalizing them. and i don't know that i can take anymore.

the last week or so i started finding big spiders around the apartment. dark black. thick. first time ever in three years. you remember. how could you forget. we really screamed. i know it's silly but for me that was somehow a comfort. the apartment had begun focus-group style testing new critters for the next folks. i figured we'd see a few of them, then maybe some moths, or roly-polys or something, and so i very nearly started packing. got real close. but when i picked up the cutting board from its space in the corner of the kitchen, a house centipede scurried out. and all the tupperware was in the dishwasher (getting ready for relocation); he looked at me, no scurrying. he stared at me. he gawked at me and said 'i remember everything'. i don't remember if my 'jesus, fuck' came before or after but before he could tell me anything more i sucked him into our hand-vac and shook him around and said 'la-la-la you can't say anything from inside there', and from within the hand-vac, beneath the dandruff and cat hairs, i could hear his little angular legs scratching and i could hardly bear it. you can imagine, i'm sure. so i ran outside, to the grass, barefoot, and shook the bottom of the hand-vac out and the filter came crashing down onto his little body. the house centipede. 'jesus, fuck' i yelled. it crushed him real good and for me that was a bad omen, y'know. a bad sign. and i didn't want to tell you but you asked and i figured it was only fair to let you know that this little death is hard for me and that's why.

in my dreams i shook him out and he had a little suitcase and he walked carefully across the street (looking both ways), and that would have been a great sign. but i suppose you can't always be sure. that's what my ex-therapist used to say (or something like that). gotta leap sometimes. or something.

your eyes are beautiful you know. it's not that i only just noticed but i caught a glimpse as you passed by and. and.

thank you for beginning the process. let me get my head straight.

he was just a bug after all.

i probably could have just taken a tupperware out of the dishwasher and trapped him that way. it worked for three years, didn't it. no need to reinvent the wheel.

i think i got in my own way.

Dismissing the Garments of the Adversary
Kalliopy Paleos

Life is a bodysuit found by accident

in our dirty bed
while I put my head down
raping myself on you
and we scream at each other
pretending I have any chance
of surviving

life, this black lace sex suit
with snaps at the cunt
the middle one always loose
plastic whore lolling open
hair spilling out in gushes of laughter
life, a nipple everybody
wants to kiss

life, surging mirthful cries
a hand clamping a mouth shut
while squalid night gives way
for the 5,037,000,659,842nd time
to coffee, to documents, to examinations
to signatures

 . . . to that also life,
when the earth merrily
swivels sunward again
rays of light stabbing us in circles
into the vertigo
of our hours

life, carousing about town
my juicy tits visible through
the lace of her bodysuit
If she wants it back
let her come get it

life, a series of lost morse messages
through crackling vocal cords
This garment her telegram to me

Band of Grief
Kristy Snedden

The daffodils have bloomed
from bright yellow
to dry petals. The azalea
buds burst over the hill,
but what grabs me by the throat
is the rhododendron unlocking
its buds. After the dark green
winter leaves, after the spring rains,
after the visit with my brother's
ghost, I come home to find
the small line of pink
just starting to show
under the hard protective sepals.
Even my giant rhododendron,
the one the carpenter
ran down with his truck
so that it still lies sideways
on the dirt, displays a slow
blush. This plant has always
been forgiving. Every morning
the bloom unfurls a little further,
loosens the band around my throat.

Tiny Broken Things
Autumn Zevallos

I often walk around
with my eyes to the ground,
looking for nothing
in particular,
but finding a streetside
treasure trove of
tiny broken things.

I like to collect them:
fallen feathers,
broken bird eggs,
empty snail shells,
bits of bone;
pieces of a whole
that were once so important
and now find themselves
discarded.

I give them a home,
or a purpose renewed,
as decoration, art,
or jewelry.
The possibilities are
endless really,
and always, they end up
appreciated.

My mother,
she's also a collector,
only, less incidental.
She always seeks
with intention, some
sculpture to place on
the mantle, or
cabinet to display
the decor she has hoarded,
so flawless, yet fragile,
coveted for their condition
so when something breaks,
it is broken.

There is no salvation
for the chipped glass

or dented metal,
but I get the impression
she finds some satisfaction
in throwing away these
tiny broken things.

Some sense of control
in cleansing her collection,
weeding out each
and every imperfection.
The power that comes with
surmising that something
is woefully unworthy
and casting it away
to the curb.

I remember, one time
she wanted to discard
my dresser because
the face had a hole
my fist had flown through.
It didn't matter that
the door still worked,
the drawers still opened,
my clothes still fit,
to her it was trash.

I thought it added personality,
some sign of a history,
proof it existed,
isn't that what a scar is?
Or is it a mark
that just mars the surface?

I remember the first time
I had known I was garbage;

it was the disgust in her voice
when she caught me with
my head leaning over the rim
of the toilet bowl,
like a true piece of shit.

At least clean up after yourself,
she had said,
and then turned away;

tired of finding the
flecks of vomit I failed
to clean, the shame I failed
to hide; the
self-induced incisions
and cigarette burns
that decorated my arms.

I left myself out on the curb.

Now, I can't remember
the last time I thought of her
cluttered, empty nest as a home,
or the last time that
I didn't feel homeless,
and to whoever spots me
on the side of the street,
please, pick me up
and find some use for me.
You can turn me into art
or something new,
you can fill this empty chest
with something true,
just please,

don't throw me away
just because I'm broken.

Drained
Sara Wilson

Like kelp drags each spill
of sun into silt,
I am drowning.
The needle drifts until it hits
the runout and stops playing.

What is a tide but constant giving
up, where even the moon
seems to let go a little.
Waves like the white noise looping.

Remind me now that this world
is round and that somewhere
around the bend rocky pools
are slowly filling
and anemones could swell again.

Sorrow in a Tavern Removed from the World, Late-January 1986
J. J. Steinfeld

A failed filmmaker, with long-past dreams
of being the next Alfred Hitchcock,
recalls his first attempt at movie magic
working in a faraway town, late-January 1986,
directing an indie film about madness
madness as art, art as madness,
nothing profound or clever
merely soft-spoken screams.
Eager to flee the set and unprepared actors
you found a tavern removed from the world
there, a deeply religious man,
a look-alike for Jimmy Stewart
in The Man Who Knew Too Much,
who, almost two years before,
had suffered a horrible loss
of a loved one deeply adored
tried to tell you the difference
between vengeance and revenge
over beers in the secluded tavern
you remember this clearly
for on the large screen overhead
a music video for "Addicted to Love"
interrupted by a spacecraft explosion
shown over and over, time captured,
as if a film trailer of Eternity
trying to catch God's attention.
Whom do you blame
no one or everyone, you think,
revising a painful script.
He wept, his sorrow uneased
by the two years,
your eyes on the screen
his heart on his loss.

you're not her - a poem long thrown-out.
Kenna DeValor

the moment i saw you
your face a faded but familiar melody
not heard by my loving mind in so long
you're not her, i know that-
but you look so much like her my heart fluttered again
like I did when I was sixteen
it was like looking into the past
of another dimension
of another universe when i got another chance
you're not her, i know that-
but the way your hazel eyes
glow with warmth as if I were visiting an old friend as if
you had left a candle burning in the window
welcoming me home again
you're not her, i know that-
but you have her hair, furrowed brow, her brilliant mind
perhaps even more brilliant.
even as you sit beside me;
sharing music, exchanging words,
I feel like I'm visiting a house that was laid to rest by flame, now rebuilt.
I promised to read Twelfth Night for you, as you read Taming of The Shrew
but I'm tired of Shakespeare and
 I'm tired of lying to myself and
 letting my heart ghostwrite my emotions.
you're not her, i know that
but when you leaned on my shoulder
and wrapped your arms in mine
 I can't completely lie if I didn't feel a small sense
of an old feeling. A feeling I thought I'd forgotten.
It nearly made me tear up
as I would seeing a long lost friend
after so long. It's been so long.
It frustrates me how much you look like her.
Maybe we'll never see each other again
After this summer is over and done,
and the decay of fall sets in,
but even getting moments to start again
was worth the hurt and I'm wiping my tired feet
on the welcome mat.
Even though this home feels familiar,
and I want you to keep the candles burning in the window,
and the music playing, I know I cannot stay.
But for now, the heartache and I deserve to sit down with you

Don't Call Until Voting Opens
Vicky Pointing

"And cut. Thanks, Natalie."

As soon as the camera dips, the fragile smile slides from the girl's face. She hunches her shoulders, hands in her lap plucking at the too-tight material of her dress, chosen by wardrobe to cling in all the wrong places. It's been decided she's the pity vote, although they're all pity votes really.

"Am I done?" Natalie asks.

A nod from the producer and she wriggles and drops from the too-small too-high bar stool they've placed her on. Her face is flushed as she heads to the back of the room, to a man swamped by his wheelchair, his body crumpled like discarded paper.

"Dad?" she says, and his eyes flutter open.

"Sweetheart," he says.

"You hungry?"

He nods, although he isn't, and she wheels him from the room.

The producer reviews her footage, lingering on a close-up of Natalie wiping her eyes with the sleeve of her dress. She laughs.

"Good work," she says. "Bring in the next one. Who is it?"

"The bachelor," someone says. The team has nicknames for each of the six competitors and their companions: pity vote, posh totty, ice twins, damn hippies, doolally Larry, and – their star player – the bachelor. These interviews are part of the build up to the live show, which will be streamed 24/7 into the homes of eager viewers, chomping at the bit to view the first - and quite possibly last, judging by the legal battle that's already raging - series of their show. It took time to find a production company with the balls to fund it, and more time to seek out anyone desperate enough to take part. The producer shut down her socials months ago, bored by the endless stream of disgusted and abusive messages, the threats to harm, rape or kill her. But they made it: they've got their competitors, lambs to the slaughter, each paired with a partner, or family member who will benefit if their loved one wins.

Getting the bachelor signed up though, that was a major coup.

The producer ramps up her smile as he walks in. She's met him before, of course, and seen his image a million times, usually attached to some delicious piece of gossip. Blue eyes with a mischievous twinkle, dark hair smoothed back from his face, chiselled jawline. In the flesh, he is something else. The producer's breath hitches. Even though he's scowling, he's still the most beautiful thing she's ever seen.

"Jay." His mother follows him in, her rich voice clipped with disappointment. She is impeccably dressed as always, her hair perfectly set, the nails that grip her handbag neatly manicured. You'd never know from looking at her, but news of the diagnosis was all over social media. The bachelor stops, but doesn't turn in her direction, just glares at the team, jaw taut.

Another row, the producer thinks. *Should make for an interesting interview.* "Welcome back, Jay," she says.

The bachelor grunts. "Let's get this done." He steps past the cameras, settling himself on the bar stool as if it's his throne.

"Ready?" the producer says.

As if at the flick of a switch, a smile appears on Jay's face with all the warmth and beauty of the rising sun. He slides one hand through his hair and grins at the camera. The producer takes care not to swoon, instead exchanging glances with her team. It may be his mother who's competing, but he's the big draw, he's the one everyone will be watching, as he eats, sleeps, works out… showers. There will be little privacy in the complex, they've made sure of that.

The interviewer steps forward, flicking her hair and extending a hand. "Mr Beresford, Jay, I'm Becky. It's such a pleasure to meet you."

The producer picked Becky with care. She's just his type: blonde, petite, great tits, with the sort of gentle beauty that looks easy to crush.

"The pleasure's all mine," he says, pinning her with his gaze as she takes a seat and pulls it close to him. A lesser woman would melt under that stare, but Becky knows what she's doing. She starts the interview with fluff, giggles and simpers through the opening questions, then her expression becomes serious, sympathetic.

"Given the difficult time you've been having recently, is there anything you'd like to say to the people spreading such awful rumours about you."

The producer glances at Jay's mother, catches the almost imperceptible twitch of her lip.

Jay smiles wryly. "Which ones? I don't pay attention to rumours. I'm sorry people don't have better things to do with their time."

Becky places two fingers lightly on his knee, a butterfly touch. "Of course, but it must be hurtful: all those posts on social media."

He leans towards her. "I don't look at them."

Becky laughs prettily, then moves on. "What was your reaction when your mother told you about the show?"

Jay looks past the cameras. "My mother has always been exceptional, always put family first. But this... this is incredible." There's no hint of their recent argument in his adoring smile, much to the producer's disappointment.

Once the interviews are wrapped, everyone heads down to dinner, the competitors meeting for the first time. The producer watches as hands are shaken, smiles and small talk exchanged. The pity vote - Natalie - seems genuinely interested in everyone, but her father spends most of his time asleep, so she must be desperate for someone to talk to. Her most willing victim is posh totty: Mariam, with her soft, ripe skin and brittle gaze. Her devoted husband is forever hovering at her elbow like an over-attentive waiter.

The damn hippies - Saffron and Harmony - are friendly enough too, but that probably has something to do with the waves of smoky sweetness coming off them. The producer's surprised the ice twins aren't getting stoned just sitting next to them. They're not actually twins but close enough in age and appearance to seem it. Both tall, slender, with ash-blonde hair and matching frigid faces. They warmed up during their preliminary interviews – they wouldn't have been selected otherwise - but the older sister Lily was wary to begin with, and the producer's certain there's some secret in her past, a tragedy to be laid bare for viewers. The brother, Luke, is earnest, engaging, wholesome.

On the other side of him, Doolally Larry sits with his fingers in his food, while his wife chatters brightly.

"I always try to have a positive outlook" she said, in her interview. They're the oldest competitors, both in their late sixties. Larry is staring at Jay and his mother who sit apart from the others at the end of the table. Jay ignores him, but his mother smiles, then goes back to her dinner, taking tiny mouthfuls, every movement of her hands elegant and precise. They must be used to being stared at: everyone at the table glances over at them every now and then. Except for Natalie.

The producer watches them all. She thought they'd look more nervous by this point, but at least the scheming's started. Posh totty and her husband have their heads close together, glancing at the others, whispering. The husband nods and abruptly leaves the table. A member of the crew follows at a distance, handheld camera at his side, just in case.

The competitors' phones and laptops have been taken away already. In the morning they'll film messages for family members, which will be broadcast as part of the show.

The next day there are a few tear-stained faces as they board the plane, frayed tempers as baggage is stowed. *That's better*, the producer thinks, as her crew capture it all. It's not a long flight but blinds are drawn across each window, the competitors kept in the dark until they land and the doors open. Everyone jostles to get their first glimpse of the complex, greeting it with murmurs of surprise. The island is small, flat and green; the complex sits alone on the side of the only hill, surrounded by beautiful gardens, a river at its feet.

The competitors are given a tour - bedroom suites, dining area, guest lounge, health and therapy centre - and then left to wander while the crew check each surveillance camera. The producer visits the control room, gazing tenderly at her wall of monitors. She clicks to zoom in on the bachelor, who's visiting his en suite but has worked out where the main camera is and moved a towel rail in front of it.

"Clever boy," the producer murmurs. It doesn't matter. They have other cameras.

She clicks a few more buttons, hoping for extra footage for that evening's episode, which will introduce competitors and companions to their adoring public. Straight after it's broadcast, all cameras will go live. After that, her crew will stir things up as much as they can, as will the personal assistants allocated to each competitor. As for the running order, only the crew and each competitor know when their turn will come. The producer clicks again, to pity vote and her father. So far they've done nothing of interest except breaking their radio mics, which was soon fixed. Another click and posh totty Mariam appears on screen, rising from an early bath, taking her time to wrap a towel around the curves of her body. She doesn't have long to impress the viewers, so every little helps.

Later, the producer and her crew watch live as the first episode airs, their mobile phones switched to silent, screens in spasm as all hell breaks loose on social media. She allows herself a fist pump when they make the ten o'clock news; the nation's outrage solemnly reported. The show's name is trending, as is #ComeDieWithMe: some small-time journo's pun. There's no such thing as bad press, as the early viewing figures prove.

That night at the complex the damn hippies copulate noisily, keeping their neighbours awake. Still, cunnilingus is always good for ratings. The health and therapy centre gets a few interesting requests, and the crew start taking bets, trying to figure out what their competitors have planned. At dawn, Larry wanders the garden in his pyjamas, his wife following. They still make it to breakfast, where only brief murmured conversations and the occasional scrape of a knife or spoon break the silence. Everyone is waiting to see who will go first.

It happens as the sun sets, staining the sky with a violent tangerine glow as it sinks into the sea. The producer approves: this is meant to be a spectacle, after all. She issues orders to the crew as Mariam and her ever-attentive husband head to the river at the foot of the complex. A klaxon sounds, and the other competitors obediently gather in the lounge, where live footage already plays on the huge TV. They watch, some settling on sofas, others standing transfixed by the screen, as Mariam sweeps off her hair, the shiny scalp beneath a dead giveaway. She changes into a high-necked, floor-length dress, her husband assisting with the long red-brown wig that hangs past her waist. Her costume.

Mariam reaches for her husband, who takes her arm gently and guides her into the water. They turn their faces to each other. A medic calls from the bank, asks if she's ready, then wades in. He spends a little time talking to her, then hands over a needle and syringe. She hesitates, looks at her husband, then sinks the needle into the side of her stomach. He tells her he loves her, but her eyelids are already fluttering shut. Her grip on him slackens and she drops into the water. The medic and crew drag her husband away as Mariam's personal assistant carefully arranges her body to lie flat in the river, and ties a garland of flowers to her hand, which bobs softly in the water. Once everyone has left, the cameras pan out, framing the scene in its full glory. The shot holds steady, unaccompanied by music or voice-over. After a few more seconds, the water has soaked into Mariam's costume, and she sinks below the surface.

In the lounge, Natalie stifles a sob, cupping her father's frail hand. Doolally Larry walks up to the screen and strokes Mariam's face.

"Too much water," he says.

The producer grins.

On her cue, text fades in onscreen: "Mariam Musa. Age 32. Cancer."

Then, a sombre voice-over: "Please do not call in with your scores. We will notify you when voting opens."

One down, five to go, the producer thinks, checking her phone. Live viewing figures are through the roof, with scores already being posted online, mainly anonymously.

6 out of 10 its pretty but not an original idea I mean its that old Ophelia painting. Also not very dramatic.

OMG can't believe they actually went through with this! 2/10 for making me watch someone die!

"Yeah, but you didn't switch over," the producer mutters.

The voting won't open until all competitors are dead. Only then will the public decide who's served up the best suicide. With three hundred grand at stake for the winner's companion, she's expecting great things. Awful, brilliant, career-making TV.

The producer cuts back to the lounge, where the others sit and stand silently. Jay moves first, placing a hand on his mother's shoulder, which she reaches to touch, smiling sadly at him. They make it look spontaneous, genuine. In shadow behind them, the producer can just make out Natalie's disgusted expression.

Jay turns to leave the room and the others follow, except for Natalie, who leans against the back of her father's chair, staring at Mariam's submerged body. The tips of her wig reach the water's surface, swaying with the river's current.

The next morning there's another round of interviews, attended by the counsellor, who stands at the back chewing gum, glancing at his watch.

"Mariam seemed like a kind and gentle woman," Larry's wife is saying. "She listened to everyone."

"What did you think of her death?" their interviewer asks.

"Very sad."

"No, I mean, how would you score it. Our viewers will want to know."

She stares at him blankly, then turns to her husband. He seems to suddenly notice she's holding his hand and pulls away, looking around urgently.

"Where's my wife?"

At three in the morning, the producer gets a call. She drags on clothes, downs half a cup of cold coffee, and races through the complex. In the reception area, crew surround Saffron and Harmony, who wait on plastic chairs like naughty school children. Harmony clutches a small, scuffed suitcase to her chest. When she sees the producer, she jumps up.

"I'm not doing this," she says.

Saffron stands too. "Baby."

"Fuck off. You would have let me die."

Saffron shakes her head. "I thought we'd tried everything."

The producer looks to her crew. One of the techs fills her in, quietly.

"Her parents found a new treatment and they'll pay for it, but she has to leave Saffron. Saffron deleted their messages before Harmony got them. We let Harmony know." He grins. "Huge screaming fit. She trashed their room."

"Excellent." She neatly sidesteps Saffron to address Harmony. "You'll be in breach of contract. Do your parents know?"

Harmony glares at her. "They don't give a shit. They love me."

"You said they hated you," Saffron says.

Harmony ignores her. "If there's a chance I'll live, they'll pay whatever they have to."

The producer tries not to look gleeful.

By that evening, Harmony (real name Deborah) has left with her modestly dressed, stiff lipped parents. Saffron is obliged to stay, and the producer makes sure she's last to enter the dining room, after the others have been told what she did. Champagne is served to everyone well enough to drink it, long before there's any sign of the food. The alcohol's effectiveness is improved with a little dash of something extra that no-one but the kitchen staff knows about. Saffron shuffles in, going straight to an empty seat at the table, head down.

"You've got a nerve, coming in here," ice twin Lily says, the words bumping clumsily together.

Saffron ignores her, snatching at the stem of her champagne flute and downing its contents in one.

The producer, enthroned in her control room, zooms in on Saffron's shaking hand.

Lily leans over. "You would have watched her kill herself."

Saffron flinches. "It's not like that."

Mariam's husband lurches up from the table. "… exactly what it's like. Fucking bitch." He sways towards her, throws out a fist, but the movement makes him stagger. Jay catches him, suddenly there at his elbow.

"She's not worth it," Jay says, barely slurring. His righteous glare is slightly blurred as he eyes the crew, dotted around the room. "Bring him some food, for fuck's sake. And that counsellor." He turns to Saffron. "Leave."

When she doesn't move, he goes to her. She backs away but he grips her arm, pulls her to the door. There, he pushes his mouth to her ear, holding her close. His radio mic is muffled by her hair, but Saffron moans, and tries to pull away. When Jay lets her go, she stumbles from the room, face wet. Two cameras watch her, the rest trained on the others. The producer zooms in on Natalie, pauses, rewinds, replays. For a split second, as

Natalie looks up at Jay, her face is a mask of hatred; rigid, sharp, furious. Her hand on the table is curled around a butter knife, holding it so tightly her knuckles are white.

The producer builds that evening's show around Harmony's hissy fit and departure, as well as the dining room scene. She throws in some nudity (full frontal from the hippies, and a hint of side-cock, thanks to the extra cameras in Jay's rooms) to keep the audience sweet. Thankfully there's barely a dip in the viewing figures, just some bitching online about the lack of death.

Fucking hypocrites, the producer thinks.

When darkness falls the following night, the crew are ready, the producer poised at her monitors. This time the remaining competitors and companions gather on the patio at the back of the complex, where a wide velvet curtain blocks their view of the garden beyond. Music blares, the lights in the complex go out and the curtain drops, all at the same moment.

Spotlights swivel and fix on Luke, suspended above them, a pale spider at the centre of a jagged metal web. His arms and legs, wrapped in what looks like rags and barbed wire, are attached by chains to two ten-foot towers with round, spiked tops. Lightning bursts from the towers, again and again, striking the metal web. Luke's body jerks and jolts against the restraints.

Larry's wife shouts above the music, grabbing the arm of one of the medics. "Is he okay?"

The producer rolls her eyes, then peers more closely at the central screen.

She picks up her radio. "Does anyone have eyes on the bachelor?"

A short pause.

"Negative."

She checks her monitors. Spots the bachelor just as he moves off camera. Switches to his radio mic. There's a grunt, the rustle of fabric.

"I have to go. You don't want me to get into trouble, do you?" Becky's voice, somehow maintaining a warm flirtatious edge in spite of the fury she can hear in it.

Shit.

The producer heads out with her handheld, running through corridors. She rounds a corner. Pity vote's already there, reaching to pull something from her boot, just as

Becky extricates herself from Jay's grip. As the producer passes Natalie, she straightens up and her eyes widen, lip trembling. Becky's shirt is crumpled, the collar torn, her hair escaping a now-lopsided ponytail. Her pupils are huge black holes, and beneath them a bruise blooms across her cheek. She turns and sees the producer, shakes herself and smiles.

"Oops, too much bubbly."

Jay says nothing, glaring at them all, then picks up a discarded bottle, still half full, and walks away.

"Aren't you going to do something?" Natalie says, pawing at the producer's shirt. She jabs a finger at Becky. "He attacked her."

The producer shakes her head. "An unfortunate misunderstanding. Luke's performance is back that way."

One of her team has appeared, and steers Natalie away.

The producer turns to Becky. "I thought you could handle him."

Becky snarls. "What the fuck was in that champagne?"

"Get some ice on that," she points to Becky's face. "Next time, get me something on camera."

Back in the garden, Lily appears at the bottom of the metal web, bare footed, dressed in a costume of white rags. She climbs to her brother and nestles into his side. After a moment, she moves away to a nearby platform. As soon as she's clear, the lightning's frequency increases. Fireworks explode into the air, splinters of white. Luke convulses once, twice, and hangs limply. A brief moment of silence and darkness, then the web is set alight, Luke's body lit by the flames but untouched at its centre.

"Well, that was dramatic," the producer mutters. She radios one of her team. "Interview Lily now, and again first thing. Push hard."

When the death airs that evening, it's accompanied by onscreen text: "Luke Bowman. Age 28. Leukaemia."

"So," Becky says, her chair noticeably closer to Jay's than Natalie's. "You two have been holding out on us, huh?" She smiles to take the sting from her words, her expression bright, her altercation with the bachelor well concealed. Natalie grips the edge of her chair with both hands. Jay picks a speck of dust from the knee of his jeans.

"You went to school together," Becky says, as if announcing a prize winner.

Natalie slumps, expression hidden behind her hair.

"I'm sorry, I have a terrible memory for faces," Jay says.

"Well, Natalie was a year younger than you." Becky turns her laptop towards them both. "Let's see if this helps."

The blurred photo is hardly recognisable as Natalie. The girl it shows is blonde, slender, with a confident smile. Only the producer, zoomed in on Jay's face, catches the flicker of surprise before he frowns, then shakes his head.

"So, it's just a coincidence that you both ended up on the show?" Becky says.

"Absolutely." Jay turns to Natalie, whose gaze is fixed to the floor.

"I'm so sorry about your father," he says.

Natalie only nods, the corners of her mouth twitching down. She manages to squeak out "me too" as Becky ends the interview.

Before he leaves the room, Jay turns to Becky.

"Last night was a lot of fun," he murmurs. "What I remember of it, anyway."

Becky smiles. "We both drank far too much. Very naughty."

Jay grins. "You insisted on bringing me those extra bottles. Such a bad influence."

She laughs.

"Clever of you to find that camera blind spot," he says.

You mean, there's no video evidence, so don't bother trying to report me, the producer thinks.

A high-pitched shriek wakes the producer. It takes her a second to realise it's the fire alarm. She rolls out of bed, pulls on her shoes, and heads into the corridor. Her crew is already up, directing everyone out onto the patio. She's about to join them when her radio crackles.

"Code black. Suite three."

She runs, grabbing a medic on her way. The door stands open, two crew members just inside it. They part to let her through, one of them visibly shaking.

The chair stands alone in the middle of the room. Jay is tied to it, his joggers slick to his skin in places. His torso is bare, streaked with blood, deep red running from his head to his bare feet. He whimpers, his pretty blue eyes barely open. His mother crouches at his side, murmuring, touching his face.

Natalie's father is a few feet away in his wheelchair. As the medic runs past him, he turns his head to the producer and smiles.

"There's no way he did this," one of the crew says.

"No shit," says the producer. "Any footage?"

"Cameras in here are all dead."

Much later, once the police have left, the producer starts to prepare the next episode. Jay's beating might not have been on camera, but they can still leak news of it. The live feed was cut right before it happened, so social media's already crawling with rumours. Her mobile hasn't stopped ringing. Tonight's episode may be the last, but she's already had more job offers than she can count.

The police checked her footage, and know where everyone was at the time of the attack. The cameras in Jay's room and leading to it were down for 15 minutes. None of the others recorded any sign of intruders, or anything suspicious, only what could be the shadow of someone in a wheelchair moving down a corridor and then back up it ten minutes later.

The police also went through all her background checks. They didn't find anything of interest, but Natalie's father helped them fill in the blanks. They questioned the producer about it afterwards, demanding to know how she'd missed the assaults. She told them that, as Natalie never reported them, there had been no official records for her team to find. As for Natalie's medical records, the show had only needed those for the competitors, to check the details of their maladies. And anyway, they would only have proved what an unnamed boyfriend did to her when she was fifteen.

Natalie's father couldn't have done it alone, the police said. Such a frail man couldn't have shattered Jay's knees, broken his arms, fractured his skull, even if he *had* been drugged and tied to a chair. Maybe they'd find evidence of an accomplice in the forensics, but the producer doubted it. She also doubted the case would ever get to trial, knowing how little time Natalie's father had left. The police would certainly never find out how much money he'd paid the producer to be part of the show, or that she'd agreed to crash the cameras for that 15-minute window. He'd told her it would be worth her while. And it has been.

The producer zooms in on the footage of Natalie that appears to have been recorded while her abusive ex-boyfriend was beaten half to death. She's fast asleep in her room, face calm, smiling softly.

A Liturgy of Shoe-Shine and Ice Cream
Ana Marie Boyd

I am cleaning Manuel's shoes before he leaves tomorrow. They are good shoes, Rockports with flex grooves and rubber soles, a low-profile heel, slightly beveled. He wears red laces, I suppose because he is a man who likes being noticed. He makes it look so easy, the stepping-down-on-hard-earth part. Nobody ever knows that he is falling. Well, except for me. I know. He knows that I know. He also knows that I won't tell anyone.

He works two jobs, at the grocer's in the afternoon and at Lenny's bar at night. For as long as I have known him, he has been a man who has invested in his shoes, as if they are a prolific statement, as though he already knows how hard he steps down on the ground, as if he already knows how worn the leather is. "I know," his shoes will say to me as soon as he arrives. "It's just the way it's going to be," they add. But they never apologize. They are sturdy shoes. They are unwavering and unflinching shoes.

I've always been a girl who needs symbolism to help anchor me to the earth. I've always been someone who needs altars to kneel down in front of, and sometimes I even need to make them with my own hands. So, tonight, I drive to Temple's Shop-And-Go and I ask the woman at the register if they happen to carry shoe-cleaning products. I tell her I need something that can really tear through grit, something heavy-duty, so to speak. The woman standing behind the counter of Temple's smells of cigarettes and eucalyptus. Her name tag says, "Charlotte." She exudes the comfort of both a bartender that is secretly tracking how many drinks you've had while still allowing you to enjoy yourself, and a grandmother who has survived The Great Depression and can't contain herself for how much she aches to talk about it to anything that breathes.

For these reasons, I trust Charlotte immediately with the job of leading me to the shoe-shine, which, for a girl like me is basically the same thing as asking her what street Holy Communion is taking place tonight. And it might seem as impersonal as a milk carton to trust a woman from the Shop-And-Go. But, when they're wearing a T-shirt that says, "Love and Grief Are The Same Thing," it isn't really hard, particularly if you are in the business of needing to trust someone. And, I am.

"I can pay whatever price. It's kind of the last thing that I'm doing for someone I love a lot," I say, my voice suddenly cracking. "So, I guess it's kind of important."

"Must be," Charlotte replied, wittingly, glancing up at me quickly from her towel-folding to locate my position in the world.

Breaking up with Manuel has made me miss my grandmother. I want her homemade rice pudding so that I can cry into it, so that I can take long slow bites and taste my tears mixed with the rice. I want a female who has lost love before and lived through it to tell me that it won't always feel this way. I don't have that. My women have all gone on.

Charlotte abandons her towel-folding to scan the horizon of aisles stretched out in front of us.

"In Aisle Five, honey, there's some shoe supplies," she says to me. She is a scholar of grocery-item geography. She then walks out from behind the counter, and leads me to the aisle.

"Yeah, here is some," she says. "It's heavy-duty cleaner. This should do the trick. And also," she adds, "Aisle Ten has all our ice cream. I recommend Mocha Almond Fudge, but I mean, we're all different, sweetie. The point is, you just keep having a bowl until it hurts a little less. That's what my mother used to tell me."

I go home and clean inside the grooves of Mannie's shoes. I touch the altar of him with my bare hands that is made out of shoe-laces and leather. And then I cry into my ice-cream bowl and miss all of the women that have ever known heartache that I have ever loved.

September 28, 2021 at Gulfgate Center in Houston
Edward Garza

Distance
Ronna Magy

Distance:
   the amount of space between things or people

distance   you can trace it under
my skin to the steerage of life's boats
that thin bloodied line
it chases Jews fleeing Cossacks
to New World unheated Synagogue brick
up staircases where
shave headed women sit
       separate
from davening men

distance   it tracks generations
down through the skin
suitcased women
    up and down
 Detroit tenement stairs

cold water flats
pipes rusted bare
counting each penny
Mason jar spare

distance   I fed my children tastes of that bread
the way women like challah
twist and fall bedding down with the bodies of men
the way women follow
    two steps behind
    in back of
their men

Yu Yi
Joan Mazza

Even now, amid this quiet solitude that feeds
imagination and lets words soar and pour
down the page without stop, even

through these contented days, the ticking clock,
the gurgling of the coffeepot, usual ways
of doing chores in order, folding towels, socks,

yet missing that element of the next passion,
the rush at touch, the eagerness of an embrace,
the kick of the unexpected kiss that morphs

into a straight-pathed drive that's been absent
for decades, the ecstasy and potency of full-
body immersion, its consummation. The desire

for all that's new, surprising, shock at a missed
truth, thrill of the curtain rising on an immense
stage. The orchestra tunes, plays the overture,

you must remind yourself to breathe. Not memory,
this intensity is new, waits out there calling, grabs
like the scent of cut lemons juiced and sugared.

To be excited, eager with anticipation for the next
adventure, what happens next. The start of a new year
with noisemakers and clapping among new friends.

*noun. The longing to feel things intensely again.
From The Dictionary of Obscure Sorrows by John Koenig.
Pronounced "yoo-yee."

Paleogenomics
Raymond Luczak

Scientists carve tiny fragments out of human bones so old that only computers, softwared with the gift of decoding the inscrutable bits of DNA, can reveal possible strands of plot. So members of this group of Denisovans mated with a few Neanderthals? And now there seems to have been a third group of humans who are indeed extinct but have left behind bits of themselves on those helixes. Archaeologists map the exact locations of where these bones were found and deduce the migrations from one area to another. What brought them there and not over here? What stopped them from going any further? There is so much yet to be told. When we collapse into nothingness, we will turn into bones and chunks of story that no supercomputer can ever decode and flesh out into a satisfying narrative. The ending of our story is right there in the mirror facing us. Each time we step away, the mirror wipes itself clean of us. It will pretend to recognize our faces but it has prosopagnosia. The earth is a mirror too. It will forget who we are.

Mauro Altamura received an MFA in Creative Writing from Rutgers, Newark and an MFA in Visual Art from SUNY Buffalo. His prose is published in Ovunquesiamo.com, Crimereads.com, Yolk Literary, Showcase: Object and Idea, and Milk Candy Review. He received a 2022 Prose Fellowship from the NJ State Council on the Arts, and fellowships in photography/visual arts from NJSCA, NYSCA, and the NEA. He was nominated for a Pushcart Prize in 2023 and named to the Wigleaf Top 50 Very Short Fictions in 2024. He lives in Jersey City, NJ.

Stephanie Axley-Cordial(she/her) is a fat poet and novelist living in Eugene, Oregon. She writes about heartbreak, transformation, and mid-life through the lens of someone who unapologetically loves meditation, eating, and drug store romance novels.

Ana Marie Boyd is a poet, writer, educator, and restorative writing teacher who lives in Eugene, Oregon. Raised in a multiracial and multigenerational home, her writing proudly incorporates her Spanish-American roots and explores themes around family heritage, collective memory, grief/loss, mental health destigmatization, community-love, and reckoning.

Amy-Lenna Bryce (she/her) is a queer woman in her thirties from Hertfordshire in the UK. She writes poetry rooted in personal experience and is also experimenting with writing fantasy stories and genre fiction. In her time not spent writing or working in a hospital, she mainly reads and talks to the family cat. To date she has been published in Ink and Marrow Lit Issue 6.

Peter Conrad's work was a runner up in the My Dream Writing Contest 2024 and appeared in Wingless Dreamer Publisher's 2024 anthology "Summer Fireflies 2". His work has been accepted by LOFT Books, Issue VI. His work appears in Bare Hill Review, the Quillkeepers, Active Muse, Impulse [b:], Folklore, Half and One, and The Prairie Journal. He had two short stories broadcast on CBC radio. He published articles and lectures in Art History for the Art Institute Online. He has the nonfiction titles Training for Victory and Training Aces as well as creative nonfiction title Canadian Wartime Prison Escapes published.

Tinamarie Cox lives in Arizona with her husband, two children, and a one-eyed Pirate Kitty. Her written and visual work has appeared in numerous publications in various genres. She has a chapbook, Self-Destruction In Small Doses, and a forthcoming collection of poetry, Through A Sea Laced With Midnight Hues. You can find more of her work at tinamariethinkstoomuch.weebly.com.

Michael Cunliffe sprouted from an alien seed pod rumoured to have been scattered in the Scottish Highlands by the sons of the notorious Ragnar Lothbrok around a thousand years ago. At an unknown point in time he found himself transported by some little-known form of alien technology to the strange lands of Far North Queensland, Australia. Later in life he became a hippie, grew his hair long, drank schooners of ice-cold beer and listened to articulate neo-Grunge Rock artists. Now he enjoys peace and quiet. And he writes poetry.

Kenna DeValor is a writer from Bloomsburg, PA. They are a current senior at Bloomsburg University studying English Lit and Creative Writing. They have been published over 30+ times and are in publications around the US, UK, and Australia. They also run their own magazine called FlowerMouth Press.

Mary Alice Dixon lives in Charlotte, NC where she volunteers with hospice and teaches grief writing workshops that include found poems, nature rituals, blueberry scones and peppermint candy. Her past jobs include popcorn waitress, art historian, and advocate for abused children and unhoused families. She is the winner of the 2024 NC Writers' Network Randall Jarrell Poetry Competition, a Pushcart nominee and former NC Poetry Society Poet Laureate Award Finalist. Her poetry is in Anti-Heroin Chic, Broad River Review, Kakalak, Litmosphere, Main Street Rag, North Dakota Quarterly, Pinesong, Please See Me, Stonecoast Review, and elsewhere.

Timothy Dodd is from Mink Shoals, WV. He's the author of short story collections Fissures, and Other Stories (Bottom Dog Press), Men in Midnight Bloom (Cowboy Jamboree Press), and Mortality Birds (Southernmost Books, with Steve Lambert), as well as poetry collections Modern Ancient (High Window Press) and Vital Decay (Cajun Mutt Press). His stories have appeared in Yemassee, Broad River Review, and Anthology of Appalachian Writers; his poetry in Crab Creek Review, Roanoke Review, Crannog, and elsewhere. Tim is also a visual artist who primarily exhibits in the Philippines. Sample artwork can be found on Instagram@timothybdoddartwork. His website is timothybdodd.wordpress.com.

Danielle Shandiin Emerson is a Diné writer from Shiprock, New Mexico on the Navajo Nation. Her clans are Tłaashchi'i (Red Cheek People Clan), born for Ta'neezaahníí (Tangled People Clan). She has a B.A. in Education Studies and a B.A. in Literary Arts from Brown University. Danielle writes fiction, poetry, plays, and creative essays. Her work centers Diné culture, perspectives, and personal narratives.

Hayden Finkelshtain is a Toronto-based actor and poet; recent work has been published in Holes: An Anthology (JLRB Press), Angels vs. Devils (Clown House Arts Collective), Stink Eye Magazine, and Literary Veganism. Follow @rudimentpoetry on Instagram.

Holli Flanagan is a poet and editor from Eden, North Carolina. She is currently pursuing her PhD in English at the University of Delaware, specializing in contemporary women's memoir. Her poetry primarily focuses on girlhood and the bite of memory.

Melissa Rossetti Folini is a retired Library Director and the author of Story Times Good Enough to Eat an ABC-CLIO release and has had poems published in Anthologies by Exeter Publishing and others as well as several short stories. She lives and creates in The Cradle House in New Hampshire.

Diane Funston, recent Poet-in-Residence for Yuba Sutter Arts and Culture for two years, created online "Poetry Square" bringing together poets worldwide. She has been published in F(r)iction, Lake Affect Magazine, Synkronicity and Still Points Quarterly among many others. Her chapbook "Over the Falls" was published by Foothills

Publishing. Diane is on the spectrum of neurodiversity and her personality type, INFJ, is the rarest in the world.

Roger Funston came to writing late in life. He writes about his life journey, his travels, his tribe and things he has seen that you can't make up.

Laurel Galford (she/her) is a queer social worker, aspiring writer, and likely in the middle of reading three books at one time. She has participated in online writing workshops with Andrea Gibson, Megan Falley, and Olivia Gatwood, poets that greatly inspire her. Her work has been featured in Perfumed Pages, Tiny Wren Lit, Anti-Heroin Chic and the forthcoming The Afterpast Review. When not writing, Laurel can be found rock climbing, talking about astrology or adding more books to the pile next to her bed.

Edward Santos Garza is a photographer and writer based in Houston. His photos have been published by SB Nation, Rice Design Alliance, and the Latino Cultural Center in Dallas, among other venues. Follow him on Instagram @EdwardSGarza

Patrick Geraghty is a writer and a maritime lawyer living in Bayonne, New Jersey. He has been writing all his life and is now working on a character named Tommy. Patrick is currently working on a novel called, "The Upfall," about a young man involved in a murder that chases him through alcoholism and ultimately to jail.

Sarah-Jane Gill is a full time civil servant, drummer, American Football player and writer living in Cambridgeshire, UK. She takes her writing inspiration from many sources including the complexity of non-traditional family life, strange stories lost to history and both the natural and non-natural world around her. She is currently unpublished and a regular reader of Writing Magazine where she likes to hunt for interesting looking competitions to challenge herself to develop new stories.

Abiding with her faithful fur babes in the the lush Pacific Northwest, **Lindsey Morrison Grant** celebrates creative expression as the ultimate healing modality as it is a significant part of their wellness regimen.

Kim Gravell lives a dangerous life which is to say she has a compulsive writing habit which leads to her spend more time than is healthy chained to her PC. This has resulted in three paranormal adventure novels, the first of which - The Demon's Call - won a Red Ribbon in the 2016 Wishing Shelf book awards, and numerous short stories published in magazines and anthologies. Kim lives in mid-Wales. She loves traveling, people watching and animals of all shapes and sizes and can no more imagine spending a day without writing than she could a day without breathing.

John Grey is an Australian poet, US resident, recently published in New World Writing, North Dakota Quarterly and Lost Pilots. Latest books, "Between Two Fires", "Covert" and "Memory Outside The Head" are available through Amazon. Work upcoming in California Quarterly, Seventh Quarry, La Presa and Doubly Mad.

Katie Hébert (she/they) is a poet and writer from New York. She holds a B.A. in English and Women's & Gender Studies from SUNY Oneonta and was a three-time College Unions Poetry Slam Invitational (CUPSI) participant. Their work has been published in Ink and Marrow Lit, Turnpike Magazine, and Ayaskala Literary Magazine, among others. When they aren't writing, you can find Katie napping, finding the best bagels, or wandering around the tri-state area. You can also find her at kmjhebert.com.

J. Inkwell is a poet who fearlessly delves into the overlooked corners of human existence, speaking through the lens of a neurodivergent mind. From a young age, she used her whimsical, offbeat imagination to grapple with a nomadic and unconventional upbringing. Through her words, Inkwell hopes to spark a connection that resonates deeply within the soul. She invites readers to wholeheartedly embrace the duality of human experience, while confronting the depths that we often shy away from. J. Inkwell's social media is available through https://linktr.ee/j.inkwellpoetry or by searching @J.InkwellPoetry.

Erin Jamieson's writing has been published in over eighty literary magazines, including two Pushcart Prize nominations. Her poetry chapbook, Fairytales, was published by Bottlecap Press and her most recent chapbook, Remnants, came out in 2024. Her debut novel (Sky of Ashes, Land of Dreams) came out November 2023.

Katie Kent lives with her wife, cat and dog. She likes to write stories, mostly YA, about LGTBQ characters, mental illness, time travel and the future- sometimes all in the same story! Her fiction has been published in Youth Imagination, Breath and Shadow and Northern Gravy, amongst others, and in anthologies including The Trouble with Time Travel and My Heart to Yours. She won second place in three Writing Magazine competitions, and first place in Fusilli Writing's flash fiction competition. Her non-fiction is published in The Mighty, Ailment, and OC87 Recovery Diaries. Her website is at https://www.katiekentwriter.com/

Susan Kolon works and writes from Chicago and Tampa. She likes to commingle perspectives in her poetry, showing moments of wrestle and worthy, leaving the reader in a hot bath of contemplation.

Kathleen Latham lives outside of Boston, Massachusetts. Her poetry and short fiction have appeared in multiple journals and anthologies including The Comstock Review, Tipton Poetry Journal, Chestnut Review, and New Flash Fiction Review. Twice nominated for Best Small Fictions, she is a Highly Commended winner of a Bridport Prize. Her poetry collection The Ones is forthcoming from Kelsay Books. She tweets from @lathamwithapen and can be found online at KathleenLatham.com.

Raymond Luczak is the author and editor of over 30 titles, including 12 poetry collections such as Lunafly (Gnashing Teeth) and Far from Atlantis (Gallaudet University Press). He has recently edited the anthologies Yooper Poetry: On Experiencing Michigan's Upper Peninsula (Modern History Press) and Oh Yeah: A Bear Poetry Anthology (Bearskin Lodge Press). His work has appeared in Poetry, Prairie

Schooner, and elsewhere. An inaugural Zoeglossia Poetry Fellow, he lives in Minneapolis, Minnesota.

Ronna Magy is a poet and memoirist. Her recent writing appears in Rise Up Review, The Los Angeles Press, Wild Crone Wisdom, Sinister Wisdom, and Persimmon Tree. Recently honored by West Hollywood as a civil rights hero, Ronna curates readings of queer women poets.

Ana Maria Martinez is a trauma therapist, writer, and artist. When she's not helping others or creating in some way she loves to go on long runs to keep anxiety at bay. Originally from Bogota, Colombia, she currently resides with her spouse and tiny dachshund in Denver, CO. You can follow her creative endeavors on instagram @ana.m.creates

C.L. "Rooster" Martinez is a spoken word poet from San Antonio, TX. He has published three collections of poetry: A Saint For Lost Things, Alabrava Press; As it is in Heaven, Kissing Dynamite Press; and Mexican Dinosaur, Write About Now Publishing. His work has also appeared in such publications as Button Poetry, The Huffington Post Latino Voices, Pilgrimage Press, and Acentos Review.

Joan Mazza has worked as a microbiologist and psychotherapist, and taught workshops on dreaming and nightmares. Author of six books, including Dreaming Your Real Self, and her poetry is published in Prairie Schooner, The Comstock Review, Slant, Poet Lore, The MacGuffin, and The Nation.

Danielle McMahon boasts a high rejection rate.

Barbara A Meier recently moved back to her childhood home of Lincoln, KS. She's exploring lots of her baggage. She works in a second grade classroom as a paraprofessional in Lincoln, KS. She loves all things ancient. In her spare time she likes to drive on the dirt roads around Lincoln. Her recent publications include: The Gentian, LIT eZINE, Pure Slush, The Mersey Review, Antler Velvet Arts, Piker Press, Linked Verse, and Ars Sententia.

Growing up in the northeast and Virginia, **Elizabeth Morelli** received degrees in English, Photography and Library Science, but always found the time to write, submit and publish both in fiction and creative non-fiction. Today she works in organizational archives and review books for a publisher, while she allows dual passions to dictate her non-scripted life: writing and travel. Aiming towards a minimalistic lifestyle, she finds that travel occupies one of her first hurdles in navigating the obstacles in collecting.

Syreeta Muir is a writer and artist from the UK who has published in Anti-Heroin Chic, Poverty House, Sledgehammer Lit, A Thin Slice of Anxiety, The Daily Drunk Mag, Ligeia Magazine, The Blood Pudding, Roi Fainéant Press, Jake, and others. Her photography and art has been featured in voidspace, Barren Magazine, Olney Magazine, The Viridian Door. She has been nominated twice for the Pushcart Prize and once for Best of the Net for her work in The Disappointed Housewife and Versification.

Olivia Muñoz is the author of the forthcoming chapbook, These Women Carry Purses Full of Knives, winner of the Latin American Poetry prize from the Blue Mountain Review, selected by Richard Blanco. Her work appears in About Place Journal, San Pedro River Review, Thimble Literary Magazine, Gnashing Teeth Publishing Poem of the Day, and other publications. Olivia was selected for workshops by Tin House and VONA: Voices of Our Nations Arts Foundation. She has a MFA from California State University, Fresno. Born and raised in Saginaw, Michigan, Olivia now calls the West Coast home.

Devon Neal (he/him) is a Kentucky-based poet whose work has appeared in many publications, including HAD, Stanchion, Livina Press, The Storms, and The Bombay Lit Mag, and has been nominated for Best of the Net. He currently lives in Bardstown, KY with his wife and three children.

Rich Orloff writes plays and poems. The New York Times named his comedy FUNNY AS A CRUTCH a Critic's Pick, and his musical comedy ESTHER IN THE SPOTLIGHT has been produced in New York, Toronto, Tel Aviv and Miami. Rich's spiritually infused poems have been published in numerous magazines nobody has heard of, and they've been presented at churches, synagogues, meditation groups and other gatherings. He sends out one each week to rabbis, ministers, and assorted friends, and they're read by over 2200 people weekly. richorloff.com

Keli Osborn's poems have appeared in Passager, San Pedro River Review, and Timberline Review, as well as in collections including Heat the Grease, We're Frying Up Some Poetry (Gnashing Teeth Publishing, 2019), Penumbra (Uttered Chaos Press, 2017), and All We Can Hold: Poems of Motherhood (Sage Hill Press, 2016). An ex-newspaper reporter and former long-time manager in city government, Keli writes and walks in Eugene, Oregon, where she also works with others to support youth literacy, accessible arts, and democracy.

Kalliopy Paleos has taught English in Saudi Arabia and France as well as the lovely wilds of Western New York. She now lives in New Jersey, where she teaches French, watches birds from the window and takes her very spoiled dog for long walks. She has recently completed her third full-length novel translation from Greek, and her publications include poetry and prose in Mediterranean Poetry and The Ekphrastic Review.

Lee Pendergrass (they/she) is an odd and eclectic mortal who writes poetry and short stories, often in a dark spec-lit style. Their work has been published in multiple journals and anthologies, most recently in the Sigma Tau Delta Rectangle. They once won a blank verse contest, and a blow-up of their photography once hung in the California State Capitol. They feel most at home anywhere they can binge horror flicks and thigh-thickening sweets, then take random pics of rain clouds shadowing streets. But for now, they sleep in a century-old house in Arizona on Hopitutskwa and Ndee land.

Vicky Pointing's short stories and flash fiction have been published by Valley Press, Cossmass Infinities, and others. She completed an MA in Creative Writing in 2016 and won a place in the 2022 Northern Short Story Academy.

Mandy Prell holds a M.S.Ed. in Secondary English from Johns Hopkins University and a B.A. in Art History from the University of Louisville. She currently trains and coaches educators in Aubrey, Texas, where she resides with my husband and two daughters. Most of Prell's work centers on the female body and loss of bodily autonomy, specifically through rape, pregnancy, birth trauma, and motherhood. She writes on the entanglement of these topics through auto-biographical poetry; seeking to articulate thoughts often left unspoken with the candor and gravity that they deserve. The poems convey relatable, complex experiences through unsentimental observations and memories.

Shelly Reed Thieman writes to befriend the wounded. She's a messenger of imagery, a mistress of montage. Her work is influenced by the discipline of haiku. Her poems have appeared in numerous print journals, most recently in Last Leaves Magazine, Solitary Daisy, ONE ART Haiku Anthology, and The Cities of the Plains: An Anthology of Iowa Artist and Poets. Shelly is a two-time Pushcart nominee, and and creates in The Tall Corn State.

Tom Russell started writing in college in 1981 after hearing a poet read some poems to his introductory speech class. At the time, he didn't know there were any living poets. After having some of his own poems published in the school's literary magazine, he graduated and took a 30-year coffee break from writing. After returning to pen and paper, he had several poems published in various online journals and started writing creative nonfiction. Working at a 911 center was his first full-time job after college, where he studied English and Philosophy.

Billie Sainwood is a queer trans poet and writer from Atlanta. Her work has been featured in The Passionfruit Review, Don't Submit Magazine, the 100 Word Horror series by Ghost Orchid Press and on the NoSleep podcast. You can find more from Billie on her website, https://billiewritespoems.com/.

Terry Sanville lives in San Luis Obispo, California with his artist-poet wife (his in-house editor) and two plump cats (his in-house critics). He writes full time, producing short stories, essays, and novels. His stories have been accepted more than 550 times by journals, magazines, and anthologies including The American Writers Review,Bryant Literary Review, and Shenandoah. He was nominated four times for Pushcart Prizes and once for inclusion in Best of the Net anthology. Terry is a retired urban planner and an accomplished jazz and blues guitarist – who once played with a symphony orchestra backing up jazz legend George Shearing.

Dan Schall is a poet based in Pennsylvania. His work has appeared The Shore, The Light Ekphrastic, Right Hand Pointing, Cactus Heart Press and other journals. His poems are forthcoming in Thimble Literary Magazine, Merion West, and Arboreal Literary Magazine.

Mary Ellen Shaughan lives in western Massachusetts. Her poetry has appeared in Gyroscope, Amethyst Review, Page & Spine, Blue Moon, 2River View, a&u: American's AIDS Magazine, Red Rover, and elsewhere. Home Grown (available from Amazon) is her first collection of poetry.

Alley Shubert is a writer based in Pennsylvania. She is a reporter by day and a poet by night. Her work often focuses on girlhood, trauma, and breaking generational cycles. Instagram: @alleyshubert

Kristy Snedden is a trauma psychotherapist. Among other honors, her work has been nominated for a Pushcart Prize. Her poetry appears in various on-line and print journals and anthologies, most recently storySouth, Contemporary Verse 2, Door is a Jar, and Power of the Pause Anthology. She serves as Book Review Editor for Anti-Heroin Chic. When not working or hiking in the foothills of Appalachia, she loves listening to her husband and their dogs tell tall tales.

Heidi Spitzig (she/they) is a poet, photographer, and crisis counselor living in the Finger Lakes region of New York with her partner, 8 cats, and a 14-year-old corn snake. She has taught workshops on healing using various creative outlets and holds a Master's in Transpersonal Psychology. She's an avid nature-lover and can often be found far in the forest, reading poems to trees or any rock that will listen.

Michelle Steiner lives with an invisible disability. She published articles on The Mighty, Non Verbal Learning Project, Dyscalculia Blog, The Reluctant Spoonie, Kalopina Collective, Imagine the World as one Magazine, and Word Gathering. Her photographs were featured in Word Gathering and Independent and Work Ready. She works as a paraeducator in a school for students with disabilities. She lives in Pennsylvania with her husband and two cats.

Canadian poet, fiction writer, and playwright **J. J. Steinfeld** lives on Prince Edward Island, where he is patiently waiting for Godot's arrival and a phone call from Kafka. While waiting, he has published 24 books, including An Unauthorized Biography of Being (Stories/Ekstasis Editions/2016), Absurdity, Woe Is Me, Glory Be (Poetry/Guernica Editions/2017), A Visit to the Kafka Café (Poetry/Ekstasis Editions/2018), Gregor Samsa Was Never in The Beatles (Stories/Ekstasis Editions/2019), Morning Bafflement and Timeless Puzzlement (Poetry/Ekstasis Editions/2020), Somewhat Absurd, Somehow Existential (Poetry/Guernica Editions/2021), Acting on the Island (Stories/Pottersfield Press/2022), and As You Continue to Wait (Poetry/Ekstasis Editions/2022).

Stone (they/them) is a poet based out of Denver, Colorado. They can be found on social media as @persephone_stone, but they can also be found wherever there are disco balls and mocktails. They explore themes of sobriety, queerness, and love in all forms. As well as a poet, they are a photographer, comedian, and cat parent.

David H Weinberger is an American author writing in Berlin, Germany. His stories have appeared in The Write Launch, The Normal School, The Ravens Perch, Gravel, and elsewhere. He holds a Master's Degree in Early Childhood Education and taught kindergarten for eight years in Salt Lake City, Utah. Visit davidhweinberger.com to read more of his stories.

Predominantly a writer of short stories, flash or micro fictions, **Lisa Williams** particularly likes the tight word constraint of a drabble. She's a cheery soul but you wouldn't guess that from her writing as she often dwells on the darker side of life. She regularly reads her drabbles on the radio and at spoken word events; she also helps the Editor at the popular flash fiction site: Friday Flash Fiction. Lisa has fully embraced social media and can be found as @noodleBubble on most platforms. NoodleBubble is also the name that she uses when she sells her art and handmade jewelry.

Scott Wilson is a tech support specialist in Texas, where he occasionally writes.

Sara Wilson is a graduate of Vancouver Island University, with a BA majoring in Creative Writing. Her poetry has appeared in various publications including Dinosaur Porn, Sharkasaurus!, White Stag, Nod, Existere, Qwerty, Ottawa Arts Review, and Event. She is a Red Seal Sheet Metal Journeyman, a terrible birdwatcher, and a constant abandoner of the ukulele.

Andrea Yarbough is a writer and teacher in Northern Virginia. Her creative works have appeared in a variety of anthologies including her flash memoir, "On a Sunday Morning," which earned a first-place award for nonfiction. She is also the author of "Artfulness," a writing reference book for teachers. When she's not writing, she can be found traveling, spending time with family, and being bossed around by her two cats.

Ifrah Yousuf is an MFA Creative Writing student at Old Dominion University. She is Editor in Chief for Old Dominion's first student Anthology, Constellate slated to launch in October. Her work has appeared in The Plentitudes in Summer 2024. She lives with her partner and their cat, Kitty, in Virginia Beach, VA. Connect with her on Instagram: @wildeforwords or on her website: https://ifrahyousuf.wixsite.com/portfolio/

Maja Zajączkowska was born in the year 2000 in the twin city Zgorzelec-Görlitz. They are a Polish writer based in Krakow, Poland. Their work differs from avant-garde, postmodern poetry to experimental fiction. Their art is inspired by the macabre, decadence of modern society while it also explores the depths of human consciousness.

Autumn Zevallos is a nonbinary artist currently residing in New York, searching for what comes next. Of the art they create, poetry is the one they have practiced with the most consistency throughout their life, providing a cathartic and terrifyingly exhibitionist outlet. Alongside poetry, they are a fiction writer, woodcarver, sculptor, painter, jewelry maker, and are always seeking new mediums to dive headfirst into.

Milton Keynes UK
Ingram Content Group UK Ltd.
UKHW011621120824
446845UK00008B/73